Lightning Strikes

Also by Gerald Suster and published by Robson Books

Champions of the Ring

Lightning Strikes

The Lives and Times of Boxing's Lightweight Heroes

Gerald Suster

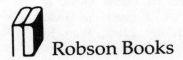
Robson Books

First published in Great Britain in 1994 by Robson Books Ltd, Bolsover House, 5–6 Clipstone Street, London W1P 7EB

The right of Gerald Suster to be identified as author of this work has been asserted by him in accordance with the Copyright, Designs and Patents Act 1988

British Library Cataloguing in Publication Data
A catalogue record for this title is available from the British Library

ISBN 0 86051 939 2

Photoset in North Wales by Derek Doyle & Associates, Mold, Clwyd. Printed in Great Britain by St Edmundsbury Press, Bury St Edmunds, Suffolk.

This book is dedicated to my wife,
Michaela Antonina.

Contents

Introduction

The heavyweight boxing champion of the world finds himself in a unique position. He is regarded as the supreme embodiment of masculinity. It is possible, even probable, that he is the toughest man on the planet. This must create a problem within his mind quite apart from troubles associated with the sudden acquisition of fame and fortune. 'You have nothing to measure yourself by,' as Norman Mailer observes, adding: 'It is not unlike being the big toe of God.'

This is not quite the case for the champions of the lower divisions, from the cruiserweights down to the junior flyweights. They know that they are the supreme practitioners of the Noble Art of Self-Defence at their respective weights. Even so, the greatest of lightweight champions knows that even a mediocre professional heavyweight has the capability to half-kill him every night. Despite this, true aficionados of the sport love the less weighty divisions and often find more joy in their contests. Some of these lighter champions capture the imagination of their own nations or even the world at large and become heroes both to their own contemporaries and to the rising generation.

Boxing champions of whatever weight have their critics,

1

who are well aware that they themselves could never attune their bodies to the physical perfection that the champion has attained through months of self-torturous training. Possibly these critics are jealous of the success enjoyed by a champion: the hero-worship of healthy boys and the profound respect of healthy men; the admiration of the ladies for a fiercely fit, fighting athlete; and the renown and riches which will grant even an outstanding flyweight the material rewards that all boxers desire so deeply. Such critics could never endure one iota of the pain the champion has experienced in his endeavour to become the absolute best at his weight – and so they put him down by calling him a fool who practises a brutish sport which allegedly offers nothing more than the spectacle of two poor men beating up each other for money and the mob.

These people miss, and choose to miss, the beauty of boxing. Above all else, they duck the fact that it is the most intelligent of sports. What does a boxer do when he faces an opponent who is taller and heavier, possessed of a longer reach and who hits 'like a guy throwing bricks'? He has to use his intelligence, co-ordinated with the physical strength of body he has tuned for the contest. He uses his brain to beat his opponent's brawn, noting his every error and making him pay for it.

Sometimes the physical equipment and intelligence of two fighters are equal. Then the bout becomes a matter of will. What is will? Many psychologists deny its existence and many philosophers admit their inability to make sense of the concept. It is quite simple. Resolve to hold your breath, no matter what, for ninety-three seconds by your watch and you will find out what will is. Alternatively, take up boxing.

We are about to explore the contests and careers, the lives and times of those extraordinary men who won the title of lightweight champion of the world. Each one of them emerged as king of the hill at his weight – a unique position.

Most of them found it hard to articulate feelings upon the matter. As a rule they were reared in conditions of brutal poverty; yet although many were semi-literate, they were not unintelligent. But the cleverness, the intelligence, they displayed in the ring was essentially demonstrated in terms of physical and mental co-ordination rather than in a ready way with words. Many boxers had no particular message for youth other than that of experience – the need and ability to be tougher and smarter and better than all opponents.

Some writers have seen men such as Joe Gans, Benny Leonard, Henry Armstrong, Joe Brown and Roberto Duran, for example, as being metaphors for their times and boxing itself as being some metaphor for metaphysics. Joyce Carol Oates, distinguished novelist and astute boxing writer, queries this view and holds that boxing is not a metaphor for anything other than itself. She is one of the many celebrated writers who have been attracted to the Noble Art: her own contribution, *On Boxing*, will be valued as long as good sport and good literature are appreciated. William Hazlitt, Sir Arthur Conan Doyle, Bernard Shaw, Jack London, Ernest Hemingway, Budd Schulberg, Norman Mailer and Timothy Mo are just some of the serious literary artists who have found illumination in their passion for pugilism. Only cricket can rival boxing for excellence of writing inspired by a sport.

Here, then, is a portrait gallery in words of remarkable warriors. They are all the more remarkable for *not* having been heavyweight champions of the world. Pound for pound, most lightweights were better than many who have worn the heavyweight crown. They managed, moreover, to ignite the imagination of the times in which they lived and fought. Some made much more money than the heavyweights. Many of their battles were more memorable. Frequently their personalities were more interesting.

In his outstanding study of English gangsterism, *The Profession of Violence*, John Pearson states that those colourful murderers, the Kray twins, had at least three hundred street fights and bar brawls when often outnumbered and outweighed, yet they always won. Yet they were not particularly big men. In their brief careers as professional boxers, they had been lightweights. Reggie Kray had been tipped by experts as a potential world champion. Crime's gain may have been boxing's loss.

It was that remarkable promoter, American Tex Rickard, who first demonstrated the public appeal of a world lightweight championship contest when he laid a golden egg at Goldfield, Nevada, 1906 with the Joe Gans–Battling Nelson fight. Both fighters were guaranteed a purse of $30,000, the largest ever offered in boxing history. Rickard placed the gold coins in his shop window. The event made him $700,000.

In no sense does lighter mean lesser. Many traditionalist experts rated Joe Gans and Benny Leonard, two of the greatest lightweights, as pound for pound ahead of any other men at any other weight. A modern aficionado, ex-champion Jose Torres, rates the Roberto Duran of the 1970s as a greater box-fighter than Muhammad Ali. Julio Cesar Chavez has broken the all-time, all-weight record for an unbeaten streak of contests (eighty-eight). Weighing in at the 135 pound limit can truly bring the best out of fighting men.

The second greatest gate for live crowds in fact occurred as recently as 20 February, 1993, when Julio Cesar Chavez fought Greg Haugen in Mexico City. Paying spectators? 132,274.

One can learn wisdom from studying the lives and times of these exceptional warriors, whose spirits, minds and bodies made them kings.

1

Bare-Knuckle Bruisers

There were no weight divisions at the inception of the British prize-ring. James Figg whose portrait was painted by his friend, William Hogarth, set up his booth in Southwark and was generally recognized as England's champion of the martial arts in 1719. In fact, Figg had greater skill with the quarterstaff, the small backsword and the cudgel, but the public was sufficiently fascinated for Figg to succeed with a fighting booth in central 'Oxford Road'.

Figg retired undefeated and his pupil, George Taylor, was soundly beaten by Jack Broughton, who has rightly been called 'The Father of Boxing'. He could not see the point of a right-handed man adopting the fencing stance of Figg, with right arm extended, and so stood with his left raised to block blows, using his right as a knockout shot. This technique worked so well against George Stevenson that the latter died. Broughton was horrified and as a result drew up the first rules of boxing.

Blows below the belt and eye-gouging were forbidden. Wrestling, however, was permitted. A round ended when a man went down. He was then allowed thirty seconds to 'come up to scratch' and 'toe the line', a mark dug in the centre of the ring. Broughton reigned as undisputed champion 1740–50. He invented boxing gloves, which he called 'mufflers', for the aristocracy had been drawn to the sport and he wanted his patrons to enjoy its practice. These gloves, he declared, would 'effectually secure them from the inconveniency of black eyes, broken jaws and bloody noses'. At ringside, noblemen mingled with the London mob and thousands of guineas changed hands on bets. The middle classes railed against it although, as Lord Macaulay observed, they hated the pleasure of the spectators much more than the pains of the pugilists.

Broughton's illustrious reign was brought to a painful end by his self-induced dissipation and the fists of Jack Slack, a Bristol butcher. Nevertheless, he became a Yeoman of the Guard at the Tower of London and died peacefully at the ripe old age of eighty-five. A large paving stone honours his memory in Westminster Abbey.

The ensuing few years were a complete disgrace as one fixed fight followed another. Wealthy patrons lost interest in being swindled. Not until 1789 was credibility restored to the ring with Tom Johnson's sterling victory over giant Isaac Perrins. Interest was further stimulated by Daniel Mendoza, an East End Jewish middleweight who became champion of all weights in 1794. He used his brain. Broughton had established a boxing ring; Mendoza proceeded to use it. He did not think it very intelligent to get hit if one could avoid it. He could not see the point of punching toe-to-toe if one could duck, block, retreat and/or circle. Moreover, he could not see the point of using the left merely to guard when it could be used as an effective punch, especially since it is obviously closer to one's opponent than the right. Scoring many victories, his scientific boxing was applauded by the intelligent and deplored by brutes.

Dutch Sam, a lightweight, was among the first to be

impressed by Mendoza. He marvelled at how this middleweight could beat heavyweights, yet realized that he was simply too small to do so himself. However, he could punch with a power out of all proportion to his weight, for he shared Mendoza's skills of bodily co-ordination and timing. This fellow Whitechapel Jew offered himself to backers as willing to fight any man at his weight. This is how the lightweights originated.

Dutch Sam acquitted himself well in the prize-ring. Although only 5ft 6 in tall and weighing 133 pounds, he had a stocky build and was extremely strong for his size. Many heavier men fell victim to that deadly punch he had invented: the uppercut. A hundred years later, this punch – uniquely difficult to execute properly – would be perfected by heavyweight champion Jack Johnson: and in modern times Larry Holmes, Roberto Duran, Lloyd Honeyghan and Julio Cesar Chavez are among its most notable exponents.

By 1801, Dutch Sam was universally hailed as the uncrowned king of the lightweights. This was not his only legacy to posterity. His son, Young Dutch Sam won all of his sixteen fights 1823–34 and was generally recognized as the uncrowned welterweight champion of England.

Meanwhile, Daniel Mendoza had lost the (heavyweight) championship in 1795 to 'Gentleman' John Jackson. Although Jackson's fight tactics had been most ungentlemanly – for he had seized Mendoza's long hair with his left hand and hammered him into unconsciousness with his right – it greatly improved the status of pugilism. Jackson brought the aristocracy and the gentry back with a flourish to full-blooded support of boxing. He also founded the Pugilistic Club to keep the sport honourable and clean.

There was a growing need to establish and recognize a middleweight champion and, later, a welterweight champion. Meanwhile little happened among the lightweights after the demise of Dutch Sam until Dick Curtis, a friend of Young Dutch Sam, achieved recognition as lightweight champion

1820–8. According to contemporary boxing historian Pierce Egan, in *Boxiana*, the handsome Curtis was called 'Pet of the Fancy' and enjoyed the patronage of 'fast noblemen'.

Corruption once again caused the prize ring to decline in appeal and the lightweights only surfaced again with the victories of Johnny Hannon in 1838. A victory over powerful and tenacious Johnny 'Badman' Walker in a three-hour battle of endurance gave him his claim to the lightweight championship. This was consolidated a year later when Hannon beat Walker in four hours. 26 January 1841 saw the most celebrated lightweight championship contest yet in boxing history when Johnny Broome challenged Hannon for a (then) astonishing purse of £5,000. The aristocracy had ringside seats. The plebeians were herded behind ropes twenty yards from the ring. After an hour of fighting, Broome's superior strength and punching power began to take their toll on the older but more experienced Hannon. At the opening of the forty-seventh round, Hannon rose wearily from his second's knee, then fell unconscious to the turf. Broome became champion of the lightweights and guided his middleweight brother Harry to a brief reign as champion of the heavyweights. Johnny 'Badman' Walker, twice defeated by Hannon, beat three men in 1842, was recognized as the retired Broome's rightful successor and never sustained another defeat. Hannon became a celebrated boxing instructor.

The prize-ring became increasingly unsavoury and unpopular during the Victorian era. The clergy railed against the sport from the pulpits. The lightweights vanished from view. Many pugilists thought it wise to emigrate to America before they were arrested and gaoled for milling for a pittance. In the United States, at that time, prize-fighting was strictly a working man's sport, ruled largely by roughnecks and gamblers.

One Abe Hicken claimed the bare-knuckle lightweight championship of America 1867–72 but his reign lacked all distinction. So did the fight between Arthur Chambers and Billy Edwards for the right to succeed him. Chambers and Edwards were both English travellers. They fought at Squirrel Island, Canada, on 4 September 1872 and the ending to the contest was dismal. In the twenty-sixth round, Chambers clinched, then yelled that he had been bitten by Edwards. Referee Bill Tracy inspected the teeth marks and awarded the fight to Chambers on a foul. In fact, the bite had been inflicted by heavyweight champion Tom Allen, acting as second to Arthur Chambers, to win the bet on a corrupt disqualification.

Chambers retired in 1879 and some historians hold 'Nonpareil' Jack Dempsey to be his successor though it is uncertain whether or not he formally claimed the title. Certainly he was a remarkable fighter, hence the nomenclature. He could move swiftly, take punishment if he had to, and punch brutally with either hand. However, he soon outgrew the division and went on to become world middleweight champion 1886–94.

Dempsey's friend, the unbeaten Jack McAuliffe, an immigrant Irishman from Cork, then laid claim to the crown. He was hailed as the American champion but there was still the British champion, Jem Carney, to be reckoned with. On 5 November 1887, these men met to decide the lightweight championship of the world. This occasion was somewhat lacking in glamour. It was staged in a barn at Revere, Massachusetts, and each fighter was allowed to select just fourteen people to witness the contest. As Nat Fleischer, founder and editor of *The Ring*, has it: 'For four hours before the affair the invited guests, because of fear of police interference, arrived in pairs at a designated hotel, and after each had passed muster, he was permitted to remain until the march to the stable under the guidance of the hotel proprietor, who led the way with a lantern.

'At the barn, the spectators found a Salvation Army group practising hymns and their presence helped throw the police off the trail.'

This classic contest, fought with skin-tight gloves, commenced at 1.00 am and lasted over three hours. Carney scored the first knockdown. McAuliffe fought back hard after this bad seventh round but was visibly tiring by the sixtieth. Gamblers who had wagered heavily on his chances grew restless. Carney flattened McAuliffe in the seventieth but interference by rowdy ring-siders and an intimidated referee gave the American respite. The seventy-fourth round saw Carney leave McAuliffe prostrate upon the canvas. Loutish McAuliffe supporters invaded the ring. Landlord Tom McKay requested referee Frank Stevenson to stop the contest before the inevitable police raid. Stevenson promptly robbed Carney of his hard-won victory by declaring the contest a draw.

McAuliffe successfully defended his American lightweight championship 1887–96 and retired undefeated, having defended his claim with bare knuckles, skin-tight gloves and boxing gloves under the Queensberry Rules. In common with his sensationally popular contemporary, heavyweight champion John L Sullivan, he preferred fighting with the gloves because they protected his fists and reduced the risk of fractured fingers. Moreover, the Queensberry Rules favoured any man who could pack a punch, stipulating that an opponent had to be knocked down only for ten seconds, whereas the London Prize Ring Rules gave an opponent thirty seconds' respite.

McAuliffe's most celebrated defence was at the three-day 'Carnival of Champions' held at the Pelican Athletic Club of New Orleans, Louisiana, on 5, 6 and 7 September 1892. Ringside seats costs $100 each, a price that would not be touted again until Joe Louis v Billy Conn in Madison Square Garden, New York City, 1946. A multiplication by forty is roughly right in terms of today's prices. Outstanding black featherweight champion George Dixon defeated his challenger, Jack Skelly. Jack McAuliffe decisively beat his challenger, Billy Myer. But heavyweight champion John L

Sullivan lost his world championship to 'Gentleman' James J Corbett, the first of the Queensberry champions. All lower divisions followed Corbett's lead and subsequently switched to the Queensberry Rules.

McAuliffe retired in 1896. In 1914, he was still sufficiently sprightly to re-enact his brawl with Jem Carney in a London ring. He was photographed in rude good health at the age of sixty-five. Others promptly fought for the right to succeed McAuliffe. Andy Bowen and Jack Burke were two notable contenders. On 6 April 1893, in New Orleans, they had engaged in the longest fight on record. It started at 9.15 pm and ended at 4.19 am, lasting an incredible seven hours and nineteen minutes, spread over 110 rounds. Both men were utterly exhausted as the referee, Mr Duffy, rightly refused to let the fight go to a finish as originally agreed and called it a draw. The purse of $2,500 was split between the two fighters.

Many thought that Australia's Young Griffo was obvious championship material. He was a most remarkable character and an extraordinary boxer. Born Albert Griffiths in Sydney 1869, he began boxing with bare knuckles in 1886, proceeded to contests with skin-tight gloves and fighting under the Queensberry Rules, and was recognized by Australia as featherweight champion of the world when he stopped New Zealand's Billy Murphy in fifteen rounds, 1890. Arriving in America, 1893, he fought and defeated most of the best men of his time. He astounded both his fellow-boxers and the fight public with his incredible defensive skills. In bars he used to stand on a foot-square handkerchief and bet that no one could hit him, always winning these bets no matter how drunk he was. Unfortunately, he much preferred the bar-room to the gym. Training bored him and he was often sozzled as he entered the ring. Although he beat most of the best lightweights, he didn't seem to take his boxing seriously; yet few could beat him even when he was scandalously drunk. In a recorded 172 contests, he won sixty-nine, with twenty-one KOs, had forty-three draws, lost eleven, boxed

forty-eight No Decision bouts and had one declared No
Contest. His career lasted over thirty years and was still
fighting at the age of forty-two. Unfortunately, he was never
given a shot at the lightweight title.

There still had to be the appearance of an internationally
recognized world lightweight champion. This would finally be
realized on 1 June 1896, in London, at an outstanding match
between America's George Kid Lavigne and England's Dick
Burge.

NOTE TO CHAPTER ONE

The early history of the lightweight division remains a matter
of controversy among boxing historians. The leading
principals in this dispute are the late Nat Fleischer and the
living Herbert G Goldman. Goldman recognizes one Caleb
Baldwin of Westminster as the first lightweight champion
'around 1795' but admits that he lost to Dutch Sam in 1804.
Even so, Goldman calls Dutch Sam a welterweight.

'Jack Randall, "The (Original) Nonpareil" was considered
lightweight champion from 1817 to 1821; he never lost a
contest,' Goldman states. By contrast, Fleischer praises
Randall as being the greatest of all bare-knuckle middleweight
champions.

Both men agree that Dick Curtis 'Pet of the Fancy' reigned
as champion during the mid-1820s. However, Fleischer had
Curtis beating one Barney Aaron 'in a fierce 55-minute battle
on February 27, 1827': Goldman declares: 'Young Barney
Aaron, born in London, won the American lightweight title in
1857, and may well be looked upon as the "world" champion
of the period.' The most likely explanation is that the
references are to Barney Aaron, father and son, respectively.

Fleischer held that the draw with Jem Carney denied
McAuliffe the world championship. Goldman thinks that

McAuliffe 'gained world lightweight supremacy by knocking out Canadian Harry Gilmore in the twenty-eighth round at Morris's Smithery, Lawrence, Mass., January 14, 1887. This was the first world title bout held under Queensberry Rules.'

Fortunately both agree that the Lavigne–Burge bout was the first universally recognized as being for the lightweight boxing championship of the world.

2

American Savagery

The National Sporting Club of Great Britain did much to lift the sport of boxing out of the nadir into which it had sunk. Particularly noteworthy in this respect was the Earl of Lonsdale who with his fellow top-hatted dignitaries set out in the spirit of 'Gentleman' John Jackson's legendary Pugilistic Club to rescue pugilism from its evil ways. They thought that the sport could survive at its best if the Marquess of Queensberry Rules were adopted.

Opinions vary about the character of John Sholto Douglas, the Eighth Marquess of Queensberry. Sportsmen tended to admire him. At Cambridge University, he was an amateur boxing champion, and subsequently he became a noted and formidable horseman, often winning steeplechases. Writers and artists loathed him as the man who ruined Oscar Wilde. Wilde had called him 'the most infamous brute in London'. Queensberry made sure that Wilde was gaoled for a variety of consensual homosexual offences against the law, for he could not forgive Wilde's liaison with his son, Lord Alfred 'Bosie' Douglas. Even his wife and sons detested him. Nevertheless, his infamy in the lawcourts is to some extent balanced by his long-lasting contribution to sport. The Queensberry Rules, to be precise, were devised by his old Cambridge University friend, John Graham Chambers, but Queensberry exerted all his patron's influence to secure their adoption among his fellow sporting bloods.

The National Sporting Club proceeded to elevate the sport, but endeavoured to do so with all due decorum. Cheering and yelling at fights were considered barbaric and deplorable and this lack of self-control was strictly forbidden. When the bell rang to end a round of ferocious fighting, polite applause was permissible. The NSC was a pompous organization but by its severe insistence upon the rules, it provided a clean arena for quite a number of notable contests. Unfortunately, the boxers themselves did not get paid very well.

It was quite an occasion when the first contest for the undisputed lightweight championship of the world took place in London, 1 June 1896. The finest flowers of England's sporting gentry were in attendance. The British champion was Dick Burge, a scientific boxer and, by every account, a lovely man. Whenever any previous opponent was in financial trouble, Burge would shower his old enemy with money. On one occasion, Burge gave a £100 note to a collecting Sister of Charity. The nun could not believe it and thought he had made a mistake. 'No,' said Burge, 'give it to the poor.' The sister asked for his name. It was a household name at that time but Burge refused to give it. 'That's Dick Burge, the champion!' cried someone in the growing crowd. The sister raised her eyes to heaven and said, 'God bless you, whoever you are!'

God did not exactly bless Dick Burge on the night he fought George Kid Lavigne. Lavigne always fought as though he wanted to kill his opponent. Born 6 December in Bay City,

Michigan, the 'Saginaw Kid' first entered the professional ring at the age of sixteen and soon acquired a formidable reputation. He fought fast and furiously. He also seemed impervious to punishment. In 1894 he took on leading contender Andy Bowen, still going after the longest fight on record. After a fierce battle, Lavigne smashed Bowen with a series of hooks and Bowen fell. Unfortunately, Bowen hit his head so hard on the wooden boards that he died.

Lavigne's speed and ferocity enabled him to draw with the fabled Young Griffo. No one disputed his claim to the American title: but now at London's National Sporting Club, it was the world championship that was at stake. The unbeaten Lavigne, who sported a Mohican hairstyle, tore into Burge from the opening bell. Burge calmly weathered the storm, taking Lavigne's best punches and responding with crisp counters that broke his opponent's nose and mashed his lips. Lavigne shook off the pains and lambasted Burge's body with a frightening pounding, raising visible and ugly blotches. Dick Burge lost his mobility as a result of this cruel body punishment. In the seventeenth round, Lavigne socked him with a left and right to the stomach followed by a classic right to the jaw and Burge was counted out of time.

As champion, Lavigne appears to have had very little interest in anything other than boxing and drinking. Certainly he was a fighting champion. Tough Jack Everhardt was knocked out in twenty-four rounds, skilful Kid McPartland was very narrowly outpointed in twenty-five, and Eddie Connolly folded in the eleventh. Then, on 2 December 1895, at Maspeth, Long Island, New York, there was the fateful fight with Joe Walcott, 'The Barbados Demon' and future welterweight champion of the world.

Although black men and women were being treated disgracefully in America at that time, there were opportunities for the men in boxing. Admittedly, there was disgusting prejudice, corruption and exploitation but it was the only road to fame and fortune. Black men were then forbidden to fight for the heavyweight championship: but there remained opportunities in the lower weight divisions. George Dixon, among the greatest of all time, became world bantamweight champion in 1890, then reigned gloriously as world featherweight champion 1891-7 and 1898-1900. His celebrated achievements inspired many, including Barbados Joe Walcott, whom Nat Fleischer termed 'a short, thick-necked, furious fighting man'.

It was bombs away when Walcott met Lavigne but there were strings attached. Walcott had to labour under disadvantages set for him by Lavigne's handlers. Obviously he had to make the lightweight poundage, difficult for a natural welterweight. Then, the fight was set for twelve rounds: an advantage for Lavigne's swiftness of attack which negated Walcott's notable stamina. Finally and worst of all, Walcott had to agree that he could only win this fight by knockout: otherwise he would lose the decision. In a tremendous battle, Lavigne took the early rounds, battering Walcott all over the ring with awesome savagery as the crowd yelled for him to exorcize the 'Barbados Demon' from their midst. Walcott amazed the spectators by taking everything that Lavigne had to throw at him and coming back with brutal assaults which tore the champion's left ear from his head, giving Lavigne a hideous beating. Accounts vary regarding the end of this tremendous battle. Nat Fleischer felt that Walcott had won the match. Herbert G Goldman states that Lavigne had Walcott 'helpless at the final bell'. These warriors met again on 29 October 1897 in San Francisco. It was another ferocious brawl. Lavigne was down in the tenth but sprang up to batter Walcott into quitting in the thirteenth. These two savage wars gave Lavigne a decision win and a KO over Joe Walcott, who went on to better things as king of the welterweight division 1901-04 and 1906; he was also a boxing tutor and personal mentor to the great Jack Johnson, the first black world heavyweight champion 1908-15. Walcott improved after these losses but Lavigne was never again the same fighter after the poundings he received from Walcott.

The former wild man of the ring appeared to be suffering from burn-out as he battled in a dispirited way to twenty-round draws with Jack Daly and Frank Erne, then laboured to a twenty-round points win against Tom Tracey. On 10 March 1899 he fought world welterweight champion Mysterious Billy Smith in San Francisco. There and then he suffered his first defeat when Smith's furious right-hand bombardment left him helpless against the ropes in the fourteenth round.

The Hawthorne Athletic Club, Buffalo, New York, saw Lavigne give a return match to leading contender Frank Erne on 3 July 1899. Lavigne was clearly and cleverly outboxed and lost his title on a fair decision after twenty rounds in which he showed just how faded he had become.

The later years of the Saginaw Kid were not happy. He started losing to men and boys unfit to go one round with him in his former days of glory. Eventually, bald, unfit and nervous 'Kid' Lavigne met one Young Erne, no relation to the champion who had taken the crown. The once great Lavigne was punch-drunk and doddery. He swung wildly, missed and fell on his face. The crowd that had once applauded him now jeered at an old stiff. In the sixth, the obscure Young Erne beat Lavigne so severely that the referee had to stop the slaughter.

Lavigne's successor as champion, Frank Erne, had been born in Zurich, Switzerland, 1875. The late, lamented and outstanding ring historian, Gilbert Odd, called him 'a fine upstanding boxer'. Erne's first defence consisted of a clever twenty-five-round points win against Jack O'Brien, the man who would defeat Bob Fitzsimmons in 1905 to become world light-heavyweight champion. Now he looked around to discern his next most profitable move. One possibility in punching for pay was perhaps to engage in No Decision contests.

These had been brought about following the most unsatisfactory James Corbett–Kid McCoy bout of 30 August 1900, which Corbett won by a highly questionable knockout. Outrage caused the state of New York to repeal the Horton Law, which had legalized professional boxing from 1896 to 1900. The Lewis Law outlawed the sport in the state – but there were loopholes. Paid exhibitions of 'sparring' remained legal: it was legal too, in these 'exhibitions', for an athlete to be 'knocked out of time' over ten seconds or rendered 'unable to continue': but winning by decision was forbidden. Gamblers agreed to go by 'the newspaper decision' at a time when a surprising number of reporters were incorruptibly honest. Most boxers did not object: under this system they could find plenty of work and publicity for more, without too much risk to either physique or reputation. It was also a godsend to champions, who could lose their titles only by being knocked out.

Surprisingly, Frank Erne never engaged in a No Decision contest. Clearly he prided himself on his boxing skill. Erne regarded his credible challengers and his gaze alighted upon Joe Gans. Gans's exquisite skills had already made him a sporting legend but Erne's edge was that Gans was black. At that time many contests were controlled by crooked white gamblers who paid or threatened black fighters to lie down for ten seconds in flagrant fixes. Even so, those who knew skill bet Gans for the title in 1900. This event was shameful. Although Erne failed to inflict any damage, Gans barely seemed to be trying at all. In the twelfth round, Gans astounded the spectators by pretending to be hurt and asking the referee to stop the 'contest'.

Erne's subsequent ventures into the ring were all equally inglorious. On 16 July 1900, he accepted the challenge of the world featherweight champion, 'Terrible' Terry McGovern. This wasn't a pleasant evening for Erne, as legendary sportswriter W S Farnsworth observed: 'With a face like a piece of liver, a chest coated with his own clotted blood, nose split, eyes closed, head buzzing and legs wobbling, Frank Erne took his place in the long list of Terry McGovern's victims.' The fight was halted in the third. However, the fight contract stipulated that McGovern could not claim the lightweight crown since the bout was at 128 pounds, five under the lightweight limit.

Erne beefed up to challenge for the welterweight crown but champion Rube Ferns stopped him in the ninth. Finally deciding to fight someone his own size, Erne gave Joe Gans a return match for the lightweight championship on 12 May 1902. Gans had not impressed Erne in their previous encounter. To his cost, Erne realized that Gans had been faking it in the hope of a straight rematch, and now he flattened Erne at 1.40 of the first round. Gans had scored a convincing but temporary triumph of skill over savagery.

NOTE TO CHAPTER TWO

GEORGE KID LAVIGNE
Lightweight champion of the world: 1896–9
Total Bouts: 56.
Won: 35 (16 by KO, 19 by decision).
Lost: 6 (2 by KO, 4 by decision).
Draws: 8.
No Decision: 7.

FRANK ERNE
Lightweight champion of the world: 1899–1902
Total Bouts: 40.
Won: 22 (10 by KO, 11 by decision, 1 by foul).
Lost: 6 (4 by KO, 2 by decision).
Draws: 12.

3

American Skills

For decades many experts have held Joe Gans in high regard. The great former heavyweight champion Gene Tunney singled him out for especial praise in his entry on Boxing for *Encyclopaedia Britannica*. 'Gans was one of the all-time great ringmen....' Nat Fleischer declared, 'There can be no doubt that Gans was the master of the boxers in his class when he was in his prime.' Bert Sugar concurs: 'They called him the "Old Master" and almost everyone who saw him said he was the greatest pound-for-pound fighter in the history of the game.' Gene Tunney admired the way in which Gans 'glided on perfectly co-ordinated feet' and knew precisely when and where to plant his punches. Of recent years, Gans's reputation has dwindled in appeal, probably because there are no known fight films which show him in his prime: but Gilbert Odd called him 'a highly talented boxer' and Peter Arnold's verdict is 'extremely skilful'.

Gans was born on 25 November 1874, Baltimore, Maryland; the town in which he died on 10 August 1910. His early years were disfigured by the poverty of his family who eked out a meagre living by shucking oysters on the waterfront. There was also the pain of despicable racial prejudice. In those days, black people on the street had to use 'the coon walk' – i.e. the gutter. Extra money could be earned by that sickening spectacle known as the 'Battle Royal'. Eight or more black youths were thrown into a ring, often blindfolded, and had to fight until only one was left standing. The white spectators then threw the victor pennies and nickels. Sometimes these were red-hot.

Gans turned professional in 1891 and displayed astonishing natural talent. He had superb fluidity of movement and a unique ability to hit hard without being hit in return. He acquired such a formidable reputation that few leading men wanted to fight him. The purses, however, were poor: in order to earn a living, Gans sometimes had to agree that he would throw a fight to a vastly inferior opponent. A flagrant example was the farcical contest against the world featherweight champion 'Terrible' Terry McGovern in 1900. This was such an obvious fix that boxing was promptly banned in Chicago. The same Terry McGovern gave world lightweight champion Frank Erne a fierce and legitimate beating. Yet as we have seen, Gans had to quit to Erne.

There were consolations: one came in the form of marriage to the actress Madge Watson of Cincinnati in March 1900. Gans also has the distinction of being the last man to box under New York's Horton Law, stopping leading contender Dal Hawkins in three rounds, 31 August 1900. One day later, the Lewis Law made professional boxing illegal in the state.

As mentioned, Gans managed to secure a return with Erne and iced him with one punch in the first round. The first black world lightweight champion proceeded to face his top contenders and beat them easily and decisively. In 1904 he endeavoured to add another crown to his already illustrious laurels by challenging the world welterweight champion, Barbados Joe Walcott, who had given Kid Lavigne such a beating and who had gone on to whip the world's best welterweights. This was a classic contest between a boxer and a slugger. Walcott never stopped coming forward, taking three to land one; and Gans kept sticking him and moving. At the end of twenty rounds' sensational action, most spectators thought that Gans had won the decision: but the referee called it a draw.

Gans returned to his own kingdom in the lightweight division to face his fifth challenger, Battling Nelson, a strong slugger who appeared impervious to punishment. This contest was promoted as a remarkable national event by the extraordinary Tex Rickard. Rickard had won and lost money as a gambler during the Alaskan gold rush. Seven years in the gambling dens of Alaska had netted him $65,000 but he wanted to capitalize on the fact. Now he found himself in Goldfield, Nevada, and looking for another opportunity.

The town was appropriately named. Gold had been struck there and one mine alone had produced more than $5,000,000 of gold-bearing ore in under three months. The more prominent citizens of this cowboy town met to discuss ways of further exploiting their fortune and drawing national attention to the place. Some of the ideas mooted were ludicrous: there would be a race-track for camels imported from the Sahara; there would be an artificial lake of beer; ten-dollar gold pieces would be thrown on to the town's streets from a hot-air balloon. Rickard, however, had no time for hot air and instead suggested a boxing match.

The Goldfield Athletic Club was formed that very day. The men raised $50,000 to back a fight and appointed Rickard as treasurer and promoter. This promotion was plagued by problems. Most spectators were drawn to the heavyweights; but crowd-pulling Jim Jeffries had retired and his successor, Tommy Burns, was not a box-office attraction. The middleweights were largely dormant. Rickard discerned potential in the lightweights. Why should the exquisite Joe Gans not defend against a tough white contender? Black versus white? Boxer versus slugger?

Gans was in trouble at the time. His crooked manager, Al Herford, had urged him to throw fights prior to his winning of the championship. As champion, Gans had just knocked out top contender Mike 'Twin' Sullivan, but his manager vanished with his purse. His record was superb. In 144 recorded fights so far, Gans had lost only five times, twice when he was young and inexperienced and thrice in obedience to the bidding of the money men and the manager. Now he was broke and therefore keen on Rickard's proffered deal. The Sullivan fight, on 19 January 1906, had been a tough one. As W S Farnsworth put it, Gans had had to be 'as nimble as a rubber ball'. Nevertheless, Sullivan damaged Gans's left eye. Gans retorted in the fifteenth round with a sensational combination climaxed by a classic right that stretched Sullivan out cold.

On 18 May 1906, the man born as Joseph Gaines entered Madison Square Garden, New York City, for a non-title fight with contender Willie Lewis over six rounds. This was a most peculiar and somewhat unsatisfactory contest, described well by eye-witness W S Farnsworth:

Well, if Lewis didn't weigh fifteen pounds more than Gans I can't tell a ham from a lemon ... Lewis won the fight with a left-hand jab. He didn't have Gans groggy. There never was a time when the black man was in distress ... (Lewis) was there to get the decision any way he could ... he was as cautious as an old woman crossing a busy street ... Gans ... missed Lewis at least a dozen times with rights that hardly went an inch from their mark ... there was that feeling throughout that Gans was the master ... Gans had the sting, but he couldn't locate the spot where he wanted the sting to land ... You never could tell when Gans was going to slip it over. One

minute you'd think it was coming, the next you'd be
sitting there wondering whether he'd gone back or not.

Lewis was awarded the decision. It is hardly surprising that
Gans rushed into the eager arms of Tex Rickard once he heard
that his next defence would be fair and square.

The first tough white contender approached by Rickard
was Jimmy Britt, who claimed something called the 'white
lightweight championship' and who was offered the
unprecedented sum of $15,000. Gans had already fought
Britt; on 31 October 1904 he had given him a fearful pasting,
forcing him to fall out in the twentieth round. But the Britt
camp had never heard of Tex Rickard: they dismissed him as
a joker. So Rickard turned next to Battling Nelson, who had
fought Britt twice, losing a twenty-round contest in 1904 on
points, but coming back the following year to KO the 'white
champion' in the eighteenth round of a scheduled forty-five
round contest. When Battling Nelson beat Britt, Rickard
wired him with an offer of $20,000, the largest sum ever
offered a pugilist. Californian promoter, 'Sunny' Jim Coffroth
tried to upstage Rickard by offering more to Gans. Rickard
clinched his deal with a staggering $30,000 plus expenses,
totalling $23,000 for Nelson and $10,000 for Gans. Rickard
promptly placed $30,000 worth of newly minted, double-
eagle gold pieces in the window of the local bank and
proceeded to contact every press and news agency. This astute
piece of business would net him $700,000.

On 3 September 1906, some 8,000 fans, including 300
women, paid to see Gans v Nelson, at the arena Tex Rickard
had erected. The Nelson camp had been giving Gans
problems. They had insisted upon an 18-foot ring to cut down
Gans's mobility and upon Gans having to make the weight
minutes before the fight, which weakened the champion.
Nevertheless Gans believed that he could beat Nelson.

The career of Battling Nelson is the subject of the next
chapter. Suffice it to say here that few tougher men ever

entered the ring. It was said that his skull was three times as thick as that of any other fighter. His favourite punch was the notorious 'scissors hook' – his fist hit the kidneys at the back whilst his thumb squeezed them at the side. He was a ruthless, dirty fighter who gave no quarter and asked none, often gouging eyes and shifting his knee into an opponent's groin as he broke his nose with an elbow.

Prior to the fight against this ferocious man, Gans received a telegram from his mother: 'Joe, the eyes of the world are on you. Everybody says you ought to win. Peter Jackson will tell me the news. You bring back the bacon.' Then he entered the ring for a fight to the finish. The spectators certainly received value for money in the longest contest in boxing history under Queensberry Rules for a world championship. The first ten rounds were all Gans as he slickly outboxed his crude challenger, but he couldn't put him away. Nelson wanted to win the title or die on that broiling hot day. Punches could be bounced off him hour after hour and he refused to go down. In the eleventh round, he swamped Gans's skills with his rough-house tactics. A tiring Gans boxed on the retreat as Nelson swarmed forward.

Nelson found that he couldn't break Gans in half. Gans absorbed his best punches, caught his second wind and came back to bloody Nelson. By round thirty, Gans was way ahead on points yet Nelson still refused to fold. In the thirty-third round, Gans misjudged a punch which landed on the top of Nelson's thick skull and he broke his right hand. Even so, and fighting one-handed, Gans managed to make Nelson look like a clumsy clot. By the forty-first round, Nelson was reduced to harmless cuffing and harmful but inept endeavours at eye-gouging. The forty-second opened with Nelson commencing a furious assault upon Gans's testicles. Referee George Siler warned the desperately frustrated slugger, who took no notice and promptly belted Gans in the groin once again. Siler promptly disqualified Nelson, who was really in no condition to continue.

'You bring back the bacon,' his mother had told Gans. He wired back the message: 'Mammy, your boy is bringing home the bacon with lots of gravy on it.' The gravy train continued to roll. On 6 September 1907, in San Francisco, Gans executed an immaculate knockout of Jimmy Britt, who this time quit in his corner and claimed a broken right wrist at the end of the sixth round.

Unfortunately, serious trouble lay ahead. Gans had destroyed his body in trying to make the 133-pound weight limit and had already contracted tuberculosis. This rendered him in no condition to face Battling Nelson again, but he needed the money and did so in Colma, California, 4 July 1908. The younger and healthier Nelson bulldozed his way through every stylish move of Gans. It was a spectacular fight of brains against brawn, of skill against strength and of age against youth. Gans, the 3–1 favourite, was leading easily after six rounds, but his pain-racked, consumptive body could not endure the hot and heavy pace set by Nelson. Whatever Gans did, Nelson took the punches and continued to bore inward, slugging Gans to the canvas nine times and halting him in the seventeenth round. A third encounter, on 9 September 1908, again in Colma, saw Nelson put away a visibly sick Gans, who this time ran out of gas in the twenty-first round. He died in the following year.

Gans's memory remained an inspiration to all who came after him. He showed his own people that a black man could be a distinguished and dignified world champion. He introduced moves that many boxers were still labouring to learn in the gyms a generation and more later. With the aid of Tex Rickard, he demonstrated conclusively that there were megabucks in the lightweight championship. His life was unfortunate and he was a victim of the prejudice of his times: yet few could live up to the standards he set for the future.

NOTE TO CHAPTER THREE

JOE GANS
>Lightweight champion of the world: 1902–08.
>Total recorded bouts: 156.
>Won: 120 (55 by KO; 60 by decision; 5 by foul).
>Lost: 8 (5 by KO, 3 by decision).
>Draws: 10.
>No Decision: 18.

4

American Skulduggery

It would be difficult to find a harder man than Battling Nelson. 'The Durable Dane' was born in Copenhagen on 5 June 1882. During his extraordinary career, he gave new meaning to the word 'tough'. He did not seem to care whether he was hit or not. One is reminded of the words of Jake LaMotta, a great middleweight king of the 1940s, upon whom Martin Scorsese's film starring Robert De Niro was accurately based: 'I fought as though I didn't deserve to live.'

'How that man could take it!' Bert Sugar observed, adding that Nelson had 'the disposition of a junkyard dog'. Nelson was twice disqualified officially but Sugar rightly remarked that 'he could just as easily have been ruled out in twenty fights'. Famed novelist, Jack London, author of *White Fang*, *Call of the Wild* and that painfully visionary science fiction epic, *Star Rover*, called Nelson 'The Abysmal Brute'. Gilbert Odd praised Nelson's 'abnormal toughness and stamina' and his 'vicious short-range blows, particularly to the body'.

The man born as Oscar Matthew Nielson had toughened his muscles by axing packed ice for the Chicago meat markets. He looked for a better living when he turned professional boxer in 1896. Soon enough he earned a reputation for the sort of body punching that could make a strong man urinate blood for a week. His left hook was usually targeted on either the liver or the kidney and was followed by his thumb. As Gilbert Odd remarked: 'The thin gloves of his day enabled him to pinch his unfortunate opponent the moment his left hook landed.'

Nelson proceeded to mug the leading lightweights of his time. When he fractured his left arm in the midst of a fifteen-round bout, he still went on to win it on points, muttering afterwards that this injury had 'made me somewhat cautious and kept me from winning by a knockout'. He first came to national sporting attention with an extraordinary contest against Christy Williams in Hot Springs, Arkansas, 26 December 1902. Nelson was floored seven times. Williams was down forty-two times and halted in the seventeenth round. Further attention was gathered by Nelson's fight with tough contender Aurelio Herrera at Butte, Montana, on 5 September 1904. Herrera's right hit Nelson so hard in the fifth round that it looked like a backflip as the 'Durable Dane' shot backwards with his eyes spinning, leading some spectators to speculate that he might be dead. How wrong they were! Nelson came back to life, climbed off the canvas and pressured Herrera to win the decision in twenty fierce rounds.

After an impressive eighteen-round KO of Jimmy Britt, during which he took everything that his opponent had to throw, then iced him with a right to the jaw, Nelson challenged the great Joe Gans and, as described, lost and fouled out in the forty-second round. He returned two years later, in 1908, to KO Gans in the seventeenth and take his title.

Nelson was not quite as crude as some have alleged. His victory over a consumptive Joe Gans may have been his greatest public crowning but he had been punching out the best men of his time. In Philadelphia 1905, for example, he had battled one of the slickest boxers of the era, world featherweight champion Abe Attell. Nelson bulled through Attell's early shots to outpunch him, and the final bell to end this six-round No Decision contest must have come as sweet relief to Attell.

Nelson confirmed his right to wear the lightweight crown when, as already described, he knocked out the increasingly ailing Gans in their third encounter, battering him to the canvas in the twenty-first round, then successfully defended his title twice in 1909. Next he signed to defend against a man as tough, vicious and unscrupulous as himself, Ad Wolgast, 'The Michigan Wildcat'. On 2 February 1910, Nelson and Wolgast met in a fight to the finish in which blatant fouls were permitted.

It was the dirtiest fight ever held for a world championship under the Queensberry Rules, which both men disgraced in an obscene orgy of eye-gouging, rabbit-punching, elbow-thwacking, and ball-busting. The bout was bloody and brutal. Eventually Wolgast, who was younger by six years, started to swarm all over Nelson. By the thirty-ninth round, both Nelson's eyes were closed and he could barely raise his arms. Referee Ed Smith warned Nelson's corner that he was one round away from stopping the fight. Nelson came out swinging in the fortieth round. 'He was easy to avoid, as usual,' W S Farnsworth wrote wryly. Wolgast countered with two hard right hand clips to the point of the jaw which left the dazed champion staggering helplessly. The referee quite properly called it at that juncture. 'What d'you think of that dumb referee?' Nelson gasped afterwards between bouts of vomiting. 'Huh! Stopping it when I would'a had him in another round ...' Nelson protested as blood flowed out of his mouth.

Nelson was always inclined to let his toughness get ahead of his intelligence. As W O McGeehan wrote:

For concentrated viciousness, prolonged past forty rounds, this was the most savage bout I have ever seen. Somewhere around the thirtieth round I think it was, Wolgast was dropped by a body blow and it looked like the end. But he was up in an instant, snarling and lashing at Nelson. After that it was Nelson, the Durable Dane, who showed signs of weakening and whose face began to look like a raw slab of steak. The features were obliterated and only the slit of one eye remained open ... it had become so cruel that even the most hardened ringsiders were calling upon the referee to stop it. Finally Eddie Smith stepped between the men and pushed Nelson to his corner. The Dane snarled at him, then tried to protest through his twisted and battered mouth. The only sound that came was one such as might have been made by an exhausted and terribly wounded wild animal...

Surprisingly enough, the wives of Nelson and Wolgast had already become good friends and after this torturous contest, the men became friends too, though Nelson was never again the same fighter. His ruling inner conviction in his own invincibility had been destroyed. On 26 November 1910 in San Francisco, Great Britain's Owen Moran moved up from the featherweights to floor Nelson five times and give him a clean knockout in the eleventh round, the only time this ever occurred in the Battler's notable career.

Despite this setback, Nelson did not hang up his gloves until 1923, though he did make an astonishing impromptu appearance at the Jack Dempsey–Jess Willard world heavyweight championship bout in Toledo, Ohio, 1919. The promoter of this post-war extravaganza was once again Tex Rickard, who had had a $100,000 stadium erected on the shores of Maumee Bay. He also sold concessions for cigarettes, chewing gum, chocolate, peanuts, opera glasses, cushions – and lemonade. Unfortunately, he sold the lemonade concession twice. 'Look, I sold you the *pink* lemonade concession,' he told an outraged vendor, 'and I clearly remember telling you that you weren't buying the rights to the *yellow* lemonade.' Bert Sugar takes up the story:

Battling Nelson arrived, complete with ghost-writer, to theoretically cover the fight for the Chicago *Daily News*. Seeking cover from the sweltering heat, he took a running dive clad only in his underwear into a mirage that resembled a swimming pool. Unfortunately, Nelson, in his overheated state of mind, had mistaken the pink lemonade tank for the swimming oasis of his dreams. Upon hearing about Nelson's 'tank job', Rickard paid the pink lemonade concessionaire to dump the contaminated contents of his vat into Maumee Bay. But the concessionaire, already the brunt of one double cross, pulled one himself and doled out the pink eau de Battling Nelson, doubling his profits for the afternoon.

Nelson was alone and broke when he died in Chicago on 7 February 1954.

His successor as champion, Ad Wolgast, was a German-American who had turned professional in 1906. He was a crude but devastating puncher, especially to the body, though far too many of his shots went south of the border. His disadvantage was that he suffered from having brittle bones. He broke an arm fighting Jack Redmond in 1910, his left hand against Mexican Joe Rivers in 1912 and his right arm against Freddie Welsh in 1914. Wolgast had his own way of looking at the world, shown when he fought Knockout Brown, an awkward, cross-eyed southpaw. 'Why don'cha hit where ya lookin'?' Wolgast grumbled.

His first defence was against Britain's Owen Moran,

conqueror of Battling Nelson, on 4 July 1911 in San Francisco. *A Pictorial History of Boxing* by Sam Andre and Nat Fleischer contains a most unflattering photograph of Moran. He is flat on his back and screaming in pain as a confident Ad Wolgast stands over him and referee Jack Welch is tolling the dismal decibel. The caption informs one that Moran had been 'belted … with a right to the stomach that had Owen gasping for breath as he was counted out in the thirteenth round by referee Jack Welch'. One studies this photograph with growing amazement and wonders why a man hit in the stomach should have his gloves clutching his balls.

The truth is that Wolgast had hit him there and Moran hadn't taken Jack Johnson's tip to wear a protective cup. Moreover, Wolgast was playing a trick used by many champions of his time, which was to employ a referee and take him on tour, insisting that he officiate at every contest. Jack Welch had been bad enough at the Moran fight but there was worse to come.

Welch was Wolgast's referee on 4 July 1912, Vernon, California, when the champion defended his title against tough and skilful Mexican Joe Rivers. This was a bloody brawl. Ad Wolgast had defeated no less than fourteen opponents since winning the crown from Nelson and intended that Rivers should be another victim, yet the Mexican fought back stubbornly. It was fairly even going into the thirteenth round, though many spectators had Rivers ahead. Rivers landed a solid left hook on Wolgast's jaw. Simultaneously, Wolgast belted Rivers in the groin. Both men fell over, with Wolgast on top of Rivers. Amazingly, referee Jack Welch helped Wolgast to his feet with his left hand whilst counting out Rivers with his right. Wolgast, with Welch's assistance, staggered to his corner. Rivers rose unaided at the count of eight and walked to his. The bell rang to end the round. Welch pointed to Wolgast as the winner, then ran from the ring as a riot ensued. It would be hard to discover more disgusting behaviour by any referee in the whole of boxing history.

All who truly cared for boxing heaved a sigh of relief when the despicable Jack Welch wasn't there as referee for Wolgast's next defence at Daly City, California, on 28 November 1912. The challenger, clever Willie Ritchie, had insisted upon an independent referee. Wolgast swung and missed whilst Ritchie peppered him with stiff, short jabs, moving continuously. Wolgast tried to rush Ritchie who responded with cool boxing and crisp counter-punching. A tiring and frustrated Wolgast was sent spinning to the deck twice in the sixteenth round, but while still on the canvas he retaliated by socking Ritchie in the groin. 'He had the rattlesnake's instinct to strike, even when mortally hurt,' W O McGeehan commented. At last Wolgast was properly disqualified: and Willie Ritchie was the new lightweight champion of the world.

The later years of Wolgast were hardly illustrious. In New York, November 1914, he was battered into an eight-round defeat by Britain's Freddie Welsh and never afterwards engaged in a major contest. He finally hung up his gloves in 1917 but the punches he'd invited and taken had left permanent marks upon him. In 1927, he was committed to an insane asylum in Camarillo, California. There he trained daily for an imaginary bout with Joe Gans, who had died many years before, and he continued to do so until his own death in 1955. The present writer concurs fully with W O McGeehan:

From the point of view of the manager, there is no doubt that Wolgast was the ideal prize fighter. He always was willing to step into the ring at the command of the mastermind, to take a beating, and to listen to the voice of the manager shouting: 'Go on in. He can't hurt *us!*' Nearly all of Wolgast's former managers have their health and are in no danger of the almshouse or the insane asylum. Oh yes. There is no doubt that Ad Wolgast was the ideal prize fighter from the manager's point of view. But poor little Wolgast will be taken to a state asylum shortly. The blows that the managers did not feel seem to have had effect upon Wolgast. Perhaps the fighter was just a trifle more sensitive than the manager.

Lavigne, Gans, Nelson and Wolgast all came to sad and sorry ends. This would not be the case with Willie Ritchie: but in the meantime he had more immediate and pressing matters on his hands. The British were coming.

NOTE TO CHAPTER FOUR

BATTLING NELSON
   Lightweight champion of the world: 1908–10.
   Total Bouts: 132.
   Won: 59 (38 by KO; 20 by decision; 1 by foul).
   Lost: 19 (2 by KO; 15 by decision; 2 by foul).
   Draws: 19.
   No Decision: 35.

AD WOLGAST
   Lightweight champion of the world: 1910–12.
   Total bouts: 135.
   won: 60 (38 by KO; 21 by decision; 1 by foul).
   Lost: 12 (2 by KO; 6 by decision; 4 by foul).
   Draws: 14.
   No Decision: 49.

5

The British are Coming!

'Owen Moran,' said Mike Tyson when a British interviewer asked him, on an interesting video, if there were any British fighters he admired. The then heavyweight champion's point was appropriately illustrated by a film of Owen Moran out-boxing the legendary Battling Nelson in November 1910. The cocky Moran avoided all of Nelson's assaults and kept bringing him up short with jolting jabs. On the rare occasions Nelson managed to land, the punches just bounced off Moran. In the eleventh round, Moran moved in for the kill. Short, quick hooks and uppercuts had set Nelson up for that. Measuring his man, Moran sent him to the canvas with a stunning right cross to the jaw. Nelson was stretched out on his back but he arose and staggered forward groggily. His face was bruised and swollen and he could barely see out of the purple puffs around his eyes. The 'Durable Dane's' punches were now so weak, they could barely break an egg. Moran sent Nelson spinning to the canvas four more times before the referee called it.

This sensational victory gave Moran a title shot against the reigning king, Ad Wolgast. As we have seen, this fight was flagrantly unfair. The contest was fierce, hard and even going into the thirteenth round. Wolgast's sudden and savage two-fisted onslaught had Moran reeling against the ropes. Wolgast shifted his attack to the body, his arms pumping like pistons, and Moran gasped. Livid welts all around his torso were evidence of Wolgast's brutal body punishment. Three smashing hooks to the head from Wolgast's left had Moran's skull bobbing dizzily – and it was then that Wolgast sunk his right deep into Moran's groin.

Of course, Wolgast's pet referee, Jack Welch, gave the fight to the champion. This was not Moran's first piece of bad luck across the ocean. In 1908 he had outscored the great world featherweight champion Abe Attell, only for the referee to call it a draw after twenty-five rounds. In a return match later that year, held over the peculiar distance of twenty-three rounds, Moran repeated his earlier win in the eyes of the spectators, but the referee once again announced a draw. Moran was deserving but singularly unlucky. He was one of the few distinguished British boxers who crossed the Atlantic ocean to win, if not championships, lasting respect and legendary reputations at that time.

Great Britain had founded boxing. America had taken it up. England's Jem Mace, who had taught the sport all over the globe, was still beating American title claimants in the 1870s. Gradually, however, the balance of power shifted towards the United States. In the heavyweight division, England's Charley Mitchell had been a serious threat to the Great John L Sullivan but his successor, James J Corbett, disposed of Mitchell in three. Britain could not mount another challenge until Tommy Burns visited in 1908 to knock out local champion Gunner Moir and Jack Palmer. Leading sportswriter Bohun Lynch observed that the techniques of Burns were far in advance of anything the Englishmen had to offer. Two of Britain's brightest hopes had been blitzed: Pedlar Palmer at bantamweight by Terry McGovern and Dick Burge at lightweight by George Kid Lavigne. Later, Iron Hague, a heavyweight hopeful, had been easily, almost casually flattened by the great Sam Langford.

It was at this dismal time for British boxing that a distinguished few rescued its international reputation. Moran, a Welshman, was one. Ted 'Kid' Lewis, born Gershon Mendeloff, an East End Jewish cockney, was another. This man fought in every weight division, from flyweight to heavyweight, and attained distinction in each. He won English and European titles at five weights but impressed the world most when he crossed the Atlantic to meet and beat America's greatest lightweights. 'Crash! Bang! Wallop!' would be the best way to describe the Kid's style. He had boundless stamina and an endless appetite for fighting. Moving up to welterweight, he engaged in a legendary series of contests with the great Jack Britton, winning the world welterweight championship 1915–16 and regaining it 1917–19. Unsurprisingly, Ted 'Kid' Lewis was the second British fighter whom that keen student of his predecessors, Mike Tyson, hastened to praise. Small wonder too that in his book, *Masters of Boxing*, Harry Carpenter declared of Lewis: 'The East End belonged to him.'

Jimmy Wilde of Wales was world flyweight champion 1916–23. He was known as 'The Ghost with a Hammer in His Hand' and he beat many top Americans weighing much more than he did. Gene Tunney stated that Wilde was the finest pound-for-pound boxer that he had ever seen. Two more Welshmen are on this roll of honour: 'Peerless' Jim Driscoll and Freddie Welsh. 'They didn't come any straighter than the left of "Peerless" Jim Driscoll,' Harry Carpenter has observed. His left didn't just peck for points. It landed accurately and did damage. In 1909 he travelled to America to fight the great world featherweight champion, Abe Attell, who reigned from 1904 to 1912. All spectators and even the New York papers agreed that Driscoll had outclassed Attell in 'one of the greatest exhibitions of scientific boxing in ring history'. Unfortunately for Driscoll, it was a No Decision bout and so Attell kept his title.

Attell refused to meet Driscoll again. After he lost his crown by a fair decision to Johnny Kilbane, he achieved the dubious distinction of being the man who helped Arnold Rothstein, banker to the underworld, fix the baseball World Series of 1919. Meanwhile Driscoll was recognized as world featherweight champion outside America. No one could beat him until he fought Owen Moran in 1913. Most spectators thought that Moran's two-fisted speed had the edge on Driscoll's expert classicism, but after twenty rounds the referee called it a draw. Peter Arnold is surely right in calling Owen Moran 'luckless'.

Driscoll's only other loss prior to his ill-advised, post-war comeback with Charles Ledoux in 1919 was so controversial that it cannot be said that he was beaten. This fight took place on 20 December 1910 at Cardiff, Wales, against Freddie Welsh. These men, two of the United Kingdom's greatest, disliked each other intensely. It was a contest for the British lightweight title and the chance of meeting the American world champion.

Welsh was a real professional who boxed from 1905 to 1922, engaging in 167 fights of which he lost only four. 'There was never anything sensational about Welsh's performances,' Nat Fleischer stated, 'other than that he was a very clever boxer. He was a light puncher, but one of the finest defensive boxers in this division's history.' His technique consisted largely of swarming all over his opponents and throwing leather without pause. In his contest against Driscoll, Welsh added insult to injury with taunting words. Driscoll was also frustrated by his inability to hit this will-o'-the-wisp solidly. His anger increased when Welsh caused him to slip off his feet. Welsh had tricked Driscoll into losing his temper and in the tenth round Driscoll was disqualified for holding and hitting. Welsh proceeded to beat the best lightweights America had to offer but was avoided by Nelson and Wolgast. Finally, he persuaded champion Willie Ritchie to accept his challenge.

Ritchie was a hard man to beat. He was a tough and skilful boxer who excelled at the craft of counter-punching. Born Gerhardt Steffen in San Franciso, 1891, Ritchie had commenced his professional career in 1907, going on to win sixteen out of twenty professional bouts over the ensuing four years. In 1911, he defeated the great future world welterweight champion, Jack Britton, in a four-rounder. 'I was faster than he was and won a clean-cut decision,' he reminisced as an old man, adding morosely: 'We never met again after that, though.'

This victory led to a meeting with Freddie Welsh, 30 November 1911, for a non-title fight, which came about by accident. Welsh had been scheduled to meet champion Ad Wolgast but Wolgast pulled out at the last minute, claiming a case of acute appendicitis. Ritchie agreed to substitute at short notice. In a demanding twenty-round fight, he became one of the very few to floor Welsh but lost a decision he afterwards admitted to have been fair. The contest left each man convinced that he had the other's number.

The man Ritchie really wanted, though, was champion Ad Wolgast, 'The Michigan Wildcat'. A four-round No Decision bout in San Francisco, 1912, in which Ritchie won 'the newspaper decision', left him sure that he could beat the champion, although Wolgast remained equally convinced that he could beat Ritchie. Having conquered leading contenders Paul Koehler and Yankee Schwartz, a confident Ritchie climbed into the ring to fight Wolgast on 28 November 1912 at Daly City, California. The best account of this fight is his own, as told to Peter Heller in *In This Corner: Forty World Champions Tell Their Stories.*

I had all the confidence in the world because of the four-round fight I'd had with Wolgast. I had no trouble hitting him. I was able to withstand his attacks and able to tie him up pretty well in the clinches ... I went along boxing my usual style, watching that I didn't get hit or get hurt, and tied him up in the clinches as best I could, because he was a rough fighter inside – arms, shoulders, head, everything went ... I got messed up defending myself. Along about the twelfth round I hit him a punch in the body and he stopped and grabbed me. That was a signal that I'd hurt him. I thought, *Well, now, brother, I know your number.* Then in the sixteenth round I said to Harry Foley, my trainer, 'Say a prayer, because I think I can nail him with a good right hand to the chin.' I feinted at his body, crossed with a right to the jaw, and he went down like a log.

Wolgast deliberately fouled out in that same round.

The new champion won praise as he endeavoured to emulate the style of the great Joe Gans. 'He was a master,' said Ritchie. 'The greatest compliment ever paid to me, Sam Berger, who was an amateur boxer and a clothing businessman, said that I was as good as Gans. The greatest compliment I was ever paid.' His first defence was on 4 July 1913 against Mexican Joe Rivers, the contender who had been so cruelly robbed in his fight against Ad Wolgast. 'Rivers was fast and strong,' said Ritchie, 'but I made him miss one time and he fell flat on his face. I was able to outbox him and outfeint him and make him miss and lose confidence. When I knocked him out in the twelfth round, I was pretty sure he wouldn't get up because I don't know if he was too game.'

Later in the year, Ritchie won handily over leading contender Leach Cross in a No Decision bout, then gave the same treatment to his old foe, Ad Wolgast. Wolgast tried to knock out Ritchie and failed. On 17 April 1914, Ritchie defended his title against 'Harlem' Tommy Murphy. This man had decisioned ex-world featherweight champion, the great Abe Attell, in one of the bloodiest fights ever witnessed. The solid body punching of Ritchie won him the twenty-round decision. 'I was told on the train going back to New York he couldn't stand up for two or three days,' Ritchie told Peter Heller many years later, adding: 'The muscles were so sore that he couldn't stand erect.'

Ritchie was a much under-rated boxer during times that were tough. Veteran sportswriter and eye-witness W S Farnsworth, writing in the Twenties, provides a full flavour of the ring in 1913 when describing the Ritchie–Cross No Decision fight:

A championship fight of the old school. It was staged for 15,000 silk-hatted and sweater-clad New Yorkers.

It was ten rounds of the old-time blood, blows and delirium. And at the finish Willie Ritchie, the lightweight champion, was a battered but decided winner over Leach Cross, the idol of the East Side.

It was one of the bloodiest ring battles this writer ever saw – a fight that had the jammed Garden screaming from the first tap of the gong to the last. Round after round the two perfectly trained youths, blood-dyed and bruised, sprang at each other in a dizzy uproar of oaths and curses and hoarse calls of encouragement.

There was scarcely a moment in the thirty minutes of fighting when both were not striking and swinging with every pound of strength. Their lips were puffed and split, great purple bumps stood out on their cheekbones and temples, slashed across with deep cuts.

Smears of clotted red spread out from their swollen noses, and at times they spit blood with every breath, like jets from a punctured artery. But again they rushed upon each other and put their blood-soaked and shapeless heads together and pounded with both hands until the mob was frenzied.

Twice Cross was down under the fearful assault. Once the champion staggered from a terrific blow on the jaw. But a minute later they were doggedly back, giving and taking as before. Their hair was matted and stuck to their foreheads in thick strings. Their breath came in thick, quick gasps. Their blows gradually lost the power to shock and could only cut and bruise, though they panted with effort to drive them home. But the last bell found them on their feet, glaring at each other with blackened and distorted eyes.

Ritchie was sure that he could beat his next challenger, the United Kingdom's Freddie Welsh, and extract revenge for his previous loss by decision. On 7 July 1914, this match took place over twenty rounds in London. The referee was the experienced Frenchman, Eugene Corri, who had power of sole decision. Bob Edgren, outstanding sportswriter for the New York *Evening World*, called Corri 'a good, honest referee'. 'He (Edgren) was untouchable,' said Ritchie. 'You couldn't reach him with a million dollars.' Nevertheless, this match proved to be controversial.

The $25,000 that Ritchie received was guaranteed by the notorious Arnold Rothstein. Was it a fix? It does not seem so in view of the fact that it would surely have been in Arnold Rothstein's best interests to keep the title in New York rather than let it go to London. Was there any element of 'perfidious Albion'? Champion Willie Ritchie was at the centre of things, so let us hear what he had to say:

Welsh was a great defensive fighter. He'd come in all covered up and work in close. I got a laugh out of it because in England they admire the stand-up stance, the erect boxing stance, and Welsh fought typically slugger fashion, all covered up, coming in with his head down, bent over forward. I stood erect all the time, that's the way I always boxed. I thought I outpointed him very easily because I landed the cleaner blows and all he did was to punch in close, whereas at long range I was hitting him clean punches. He had his gloves in front of his face and you couldn't score cleanly with the gloves there so I started hitting him on the side to try and wear him down ... That was his defence, to bang away in close ... he kept his gloves up and his chin down. I knocked him down in the twelfth round, and he probably never forgot that. I hit him on the chin. He was in there to stay twenty rounds and do the best he could ... I said to Eugene Corri, 'What's your decision?' He said, 'Welsh'.

Referee Corri awarded the decision and the world lightweight championship to Welsh by a quarter of a point.

Ritchie may have lost his title but he retained his honour in his subsequent activities. He challenged champion Fredde Welsh to a third match. Welsh offered him a ten-round No Decision contest which Ritchie accepted. He could win only if he knocked out Welsh, a virtually impossible feat, though Ritchie claimed to have won the encounter.

After serving in the US Army during the First World War, Ritchie returned to the ring in February 1919 to fight a No Decision four-rounder with Benny Leonard, thought to be among the greatest of all time. 'I won a newspaper decision by all the writers,' Ritchie stated. 'I outboxed him as fast as he was and hurt him with a good right-hand punch ... I just took the offensive away from Leonard and never let him get settled. Kept on top of him, banging away at him.'

Whilst on honeymoon, a reluctant Ritchie was persuaded by a purse of $10,000 to face Benny Leonard again in a No Decision bout scheduled for eight rounds on 28 April 1919, Newark, New Jersey. A peaceable, untrained and happily married Ritchie was stopped in the eighth by Leonard for the one and only time of his notable career. He made intermittent comebacks to the ring but finally hung up his gloves after three straight wins in 1927 at the age of thirty-six. His subsequent activities were multifarious. His Chevrolet agency in Oakland failed but his tyre agency succeeded and his apartment building in San Francisco gave him a useful income. He continued to serve boxing, being available as a strict and capable referee, and he also promoted fights. He hated corruption and was able to crusade against it through his appointment as Assistant Chief Inspector of the California Athletic Commission 1934–7, then as Chief Inspector until his retirement in 1962. Everyone agrees that he did his utmost to clean up the sport and get rid of gangsterism, all the while fighting for a fair deal for the boxers. His marriage lasted more than fifty years, with his wife Ethel bearing him two children who produced seven grandchildren. The last known report of Peter Heller had him living comfortably with his wife in Millbrae, a San Francisco suburb, where at the age of eighty, he still enjoyed golf and lawn bowling. Declared Ritchie:

> Boxing was very good to me. The most wonderful thing that ever happened to me. I wouldn't've gone to London if I had to do it over again. Boxing is a great sport, but it must be controlled and must be handled … The crooks must be kept out of it … It's a good sport and it'll make many a boy rich who might not otherwise have the ability to make very much in life as he can in boxing, like in all other sports. So I'm for it hook, line and sinker.

His rival, Freddie Welsh, would no doubt have agreed with Ritchie here, if on nothing else. In order to meet Ritchie for the title shot he'd been chasing for years, Welsh had had to stump up $500 of his own money to meet the sum guaranteed to Ritchie. There was chagrin among the Americans that the crown had gone overseas. The new champion promptly set sail for the USA where he had already won so many contests against top contenders, and proceeded to use and abuse the system in the way it had earlier treated him. He agreed to fight all comers under American No Decision rules. No one could knock out Freddie Welsh, even when he was having an off-day, and so for three years he piled up an impressive record of unscathed defences. Eventually, on 29 May 1917, in New York City, he faced top contender Benny Leonard for a third No Decision contest.

This championship match was intriguing. No top lightweight had managed to clip Freddie Welsh with a solid shot: yet the same was true of Benny Leonard. For round after round, these men tried to figure out each other's games of mind, body and spirit. Then Leonard struck swiftly in the ninth round. Welsh was dropped three times and was helpless against the ropes when the referee rightly halted the bout.

After that, it was all downhill for Freddie Welsh. He could not find the stability of Willie Ritchie. He lost his money on a health farm venture and died when he was only forty-one. Nevertheless, his name lives on among aficionados, for he was one of the British who beat the Americans at what they had made their own game. It would be quite a while before the likes of him and his glorious contemporaries would receive such international recognition again.

NOTE TO CHAPTER FIVE

WILLIE RITCHIE
Lightweight champion of the world: 1912–14
Total bouts: 71.
Won: 36 (8 by KO; 27 by decision; 1 by foul).
Lost: 9 (1 by KO; 8 by decision).
Draws: 4.
No Decision: 22.

FREDDIE WELSH
    Lightweight champion of the world: 1914–17
    Total bouts: 167.
    Won: 77 (24 by KO; 50 by decision; 3 by foul).
    Lost: 4 (1 by KO; 3 by decision).
    Draws: 7.
    No Decision: 79.

6

Jewel of the Ghetto

Some have called Benny Leonard of New York City the greatest boxer of all time. During his own glorious reign, however, most old-timers appreciated his skills but ranked him behind Joe Gans. 'Gans would have beaten Leonard,' said Elbows McFadden, who had fought Gans three times and had beaten him once. Yet McFadden admitted that he had never seen Leonard fight. By contrast, one veteran West Coast sportswriter opined: 'Gans could have called the round and the punch against Leonard,' yet he had never seen Gans fight. Leonard's verdict? 'I don't know whether I could have licked Gans or not – and neither does anybody else. But if they have to dig up a dead one to lick me, I'm satisfied.'

Benny Leiner, to give him his real name, was born on the East Side of New York on 7 April 1896. His early years saw plenty of street-fighting against antisemites. 'Us Jewish kids had to be ready for them, and we were – with bats, rocks and fists,' Leonard said in later years. Benny entered the professional ring in 1911 and displayed astonishing natural talent. He had a swift left jab and a numbing right and he could put these together in crunching combinations. Legendary trainer Ray Arcel, who only died recently and who trained Leonard in the Thirties, has remarked on Benny's 'great mental energy'. Nevertheless, to coin the phrase used by Disraeli, he had a hard time in 'climbing to the top of the greasy pole'.

Benny changed his surname because he didn't want his mother to find out that he was going boxing. She wanted him to get a job in a printing shop. 'That didn't last long because I showed up one morning with a black eye and they told me I would have to quit fighting or quit the job,' Leonard reminisced. 'So I quit the job and went home and told my mother I had been fired.' Leonard was truly sent packing on the March night of 1912 when he met Jersey City's experienced Joe Shugrue at Brown's Gymnasium, a firetrap of an old building on Sixth Avenue and Twenty-third Street. During the introductions, Shugrue roared, 'Goodbye, Benny!' and sent him into dreamland in the fourth. A year later, the red-headed, hardened veteran and lightweight champion of Canada, Frankie Fleming, flattened him in the fifth. Enough, one might think, to make this nice seventeen-year-old Jewish boy leave the ring: but Leonard had the mental strength to learn from his mistakes and so he bounced back. Aside from a disqualification loss in dubious circumstances, he would not be beaten again for the next nineteen years.

True, he experienced anxious moments on his long march to the title. There were many sensational lightweights at the time and Leonard agreed to fight all of them. Tough and crafty Johnny Dundee battled Leonard eight times in No Decision bouts 1914–20. There was also the matter of his arch rival, Ritchie Mitchell, a wicked puncher and a slick boxer. On the train to fight Mitchell in Milwaukee, Leonard told his manager, Billy Gibson, 'I'm going to stay in bed until we get there, Gib. I haven't been able to sleep all night. I've got terrible pains in my belly.' 'Why didn't you tell me before?' Gibson demanded: 'I'll have the fight postponed.' 'No,' Leonard answered, 'I'll be all right.' 'Are you all right?' Gibson asked anxiously in the dressing-room before the fight. 'No,' said Benny, 'I still feel lousy. I don't think I can go ten rounds tonight. I'll have to knock him out.' He did precisely that to the hitherto undefeated Mitchell, swiping the crowd's favourite away in the seventh round.

This victory led to his title contest with awkward Freddie Welsh. Leonard was the one and only man ever to knock out this outstanding Welshman. As new champion, he proceeded to establish himself as a living legend. He could box with boxers and punch with sluggers. When it suited the gamblers who were backing him, he could call the round and make it 'whisker close'. He also talked sense, declaring:

The fighters must be better now than they were in the old days because there are more of them, they are better schooled and in better shape and the competition is keener. I'm the lightweight champion of the world, yet there isn't a kid training here who couldn't take me out in the gym and raise hell with me – for a couple of rounds. I didn't see the bully boys they talk about but I keep hearing stories like this: 'Why, he was drunk for two weeks before the fight, laying around in dives, but he got there and won at the end of twenty-five rounds! What a fighter!' All I can say is that he must have been pretty good – but what kind of guy was he fighting? If I fought a fellow who had been drunk for two weeks, and I couldn't knock him out in a round or two, I'd be ashamed to sign my name Benny Leonard.

On 25 July 1917, the new world lightweight champion put his crown on the line against world featherweight champion,

Johnny Kilbane. Kilbane was a serious threat. In a ring career that lasted 1907–23, spread over 141 contests, he lost only four times. He had beaten the great Abe Attell in 1912 and incredibly enough, he ruled his division until 1923, when he was knocked out by Frenchman Eugene Criqui. Kilbane was an exceptionally scientific boxer but Leonard just iced him in the third round.

Having scored twenty-eight wins without a loss during the year, the champion looked around for credible contenders. Here his ambitions were assisted by promoter Tex Rickard who had once more taken centre stage and who was responsible for creating a financially golden era in boxing during what Nat Fleischer called 'the Fabulous Twenties'. Rickard's major attraction was heavyweight champion Jack Dempsey and he used him to create five million-dollar live gates. This stimulated tremendous interest in the sport and Benny Leonard was a principal beneficiary. Rickard made it fashionable to be seen at 'the fights' and women started to attend in growing numbers. Many liked slim Benny Leonard.

The Walker Law had made boxing legal in New York state and now there was a seemingly endless appetite for the Noble Art. Leonard supplied this demand when he fought Charley White on 5 July 1920 at Benton Harbour, Michigan. White was renowned as the deadliest left hooker most aficionados had ever seen. Leonard managed to avoid the blow until the fifth, when he was suddenly caught by White's lethal shot and went sprawling through the ropes and out of the ring. It looked as though he would be added to the list of Charley White's forty-one KO victims. Yet Benny beat the count and crawled back through the ropes. He was dazed but he used his ringcraft to survive the round. Once his brain had cleared, he came out to slaughter White, stopping him in the ninth round.

A great contest took place in New York on 14 January 1921 when Leonard faced his old antagonist, Ritchie Mitchell, in the old Madison Square Garden. Promoter Tex Rickard ensured that 'the cream of society' was present. This included an investor, Miss Anne Morgan, sister of the banker J P Morgan, and some of the money raised at the gate went to help restore areas of France which had been destroyed in the First World War. Governor Al Smith, 'The Happy Warrior', was also present at ringside; yet curiously enough, this was the one and only recorded time when this man from the East Side ever graced a boxing match with his presence. Also present was financier Arnold Rothstein, a friend of Leonard. Rumour had it that he had bet heavily on Leonard to win by first-round knockout.

Whatever the truth, the fact is that Benny went all out to finish Mitchell in the opening round. He sent Mitchell crashing to the canvas three times. Mitchell, dazed, hurt and bleeding, nevertheless arose and piled back into Leonard, smashing his jaw with a perfect left hook. Leonard somehow managed to haul himself to his feet at the count of nine. He swayed unsteadily against the ropes. Then he dared Mitchell to 'come in and mix it'. Mitchell suspected a trick and stayed away. It was indeed a trick – a trick that gave Benny time to recover. Once his senses had cleared, he came out for the second round to take Mitchell to the cleaners. It was a piece of methodical destruction. According to Nat Fleischer, Leonard came back 'like a fighting wildcat' and decked Mitchell three more times before he put him to bed in the sixth round.

Leonard's next fight was less glorious. He stepped up to the welterweight division to challenge its champion, the great Jack Britton, at the New York Velodrome, 26 June 1922. Benny's performance was curiously lacklustre that night. Some blamed his friend, the gangster Arnold Rothstein. Although Leonard was the bookies' favourite, he boxed feebly. Britton piled up the points. In the thirteenth round, Leonard suddenly sank in a body shot and Britton dropped to one knee, protesting to the referee that the blow had been low. Referee Patsy Haley ignored the protest and continued to count over Britton, whereupon Leonard walked across the ring and belted Britton as he was sitting on the canvas. Benny was promptly disqualified. This was no great night for the fight game.

Returning to his own division, Leonard earned rather more respect in his two contests with Lew Tendler, a hard-punching Philadelphia southpaw who could have been world champion in any other era. This fight was held in 'the House that Tex built', Boyle's Thirty Acres, Jersey City, 27 July 1922. Leonard was his usual confident self, having twice defeated future champion Rocky Kansas earlier in the year, once by decision and again by a fair eight-round stoppage. However, Tendler offered very stiff resistance. In the eighth round he drove in a body blow which paralysed Leonard's legs. Leonard said something to Tendler at that crucial moment which caused him to hesitate, ponder, back away. What was it?

'He said something to me,' Tendler stated afterwards. 'It distracted me … With the crowd yelling and everything, I couldn't hear very good. But just by talking, he distracted me.' Leonard went on to outbox Tendler to a twelve-round No Decision. But what were his magic words? 'Is that as hard as you can hit?' he told some newsmen. 'I told him a bedtime story,' was his answer to others. 'Keep them up,' was the story he told to Nat Fleischer, who thought that Lew Tendler had stopped to argue about the legitimacy of his blow. 'I'm not sure,' Benny Leonard admitted in later years to Frank Graham. 'The point was that he thought I was hurt, which I was, and that I wanted to con him, which I did. All I had to do was to get his mind off hitting me again, at least for a couple of seconds, or until I could pull myself together – and he fell for it.'

In their return match at Yankee Stadium, 24 July 1923, Leonard turned in one of his most dazzling performances. Tendler never stopped coming forward and punching but he was no match for the champion at his best. Leonard was so far ahead in the closing rounds that some thought he was carrying his foe and couldn't bring himself to knock him out. It was certainly a superb win by decision for a superior boxer but Leonard was having trouble with his hands. 'They were puffed and angry looking,' Frank Graham wrote after seeing Leonard on the following morning; 'the skin on his knuckles was scuffed and peeled back.' 'Remember,' said Benny Leonard, 'that under the gloves, my hands were bandaged and taped. That guy has the hardest chin I ever hit.'

It is hardly surprising that after being slaughtered by Harry Greb, future world heavyweight champion Gene Tunney hired Benny Leonard to teach him the finer points of pugilism, especially all the dirty tricks Greb had used to take away his American light-heavyweight title, and the counters to these horrible and messy tricks. Leonard's tuition was so successful that Tunney regained his crown from Greb, then gave him two sound beatings before going on to defeat Jack Dempsey.

Leonard had now beaten every contender in what Nat Fleischer called 'a field of the greatest lightweights that ever appeared at one time in the division'. By January 1925, when he announced his retirement, he had also taken the measure of Ever Hammer (KO–12), Leo Johnson, Ritchie Mitchell, Lew Tendler, Rocky Kansas, Johnny Dundee, Charley White, Joe Welling in a gruelling contest (KO–14) and Pal Moran. His sprained thumb was refusing to heal and he was experiencing increasing trouble with his brittle hands. His mother kept nagging him to give up boxing. Actually, it was a sensible time to quit when well ahead. He was rich and famous and only twenty-nine. He installed his family in plush West End Avenue and paid for everything as he led the pleasant life of the established warrior who has become a gentleman of leisure.

Disaster struck with the Wall Street Crash of 1929. Benny had been so sure that his investments were safe. In common with so many others who trusted the system, he found that his life savings had been wiped out overnight. In later years, Leonard asked:

Do you know why most fighters go broke? I'll tell you. They're poor kids to begin with or they wouldn't be fighters. Then, all of a sudden, they've got money. Once they're on top, their relatives quit working. All they want from him is rent money, eating money and the price of a new set of tires. Whose advice can the fighter ask? The advice of the one closest to him, his manager ... The first thing he told me to do when I won the title was to buy race horses. So I did. Six of them. They couldn't win a race. They couldn't even place or show. But they could eat ... Who'd pay me anything for them?

Leonard tried to recoup his fallen fortunes by making an ill-advised comeback to the ring. His compulsive generosity had further depleted what little he had left. He lamented:

Pretty soon I have a dozen guys around. Naturally I pick up the check. Or, if, as rarely happens, I get through the meal alone, can I give the waiter an ordinary tip? Of course not. If I don't give him a five-dollar tip, he tells everybody: 'Benny Leonard is a cheapskate.'

Fighting as a flabby welterweight, with a bald spot dyed black, Leonard proceeded to defeat minor fighters in minor clubs for minor pay. On 7 October 1932, in New York, he was thrown into the ring as cannon fodder for that great young tiger, Jimmy McLarnin. This daunting prospect did not frighten Leonard. After all, he reasoned to himself, he might be getting on in years at the age of thirty-six, but he was coming off a comeback streak of eighteen wins and one draw, including a fine two-round knockout over leading contender, Pal Silvers. On this night, though, he proved himself to be an easy mark for McLarnin's swift fists. Leonard won the first round in former grand style but subsequently could not cope with the younger man's unrelenting and furious two-fisted assault. He was counted out in the sixth round.

After that, he tried various schemes to make ends meet. In 1943, he became a licenced referee, a job at which he excelled. Unfortunately, as he was refereeing a fight at New York's St Nicholas Arena, 17 April 1947, he suddenly crumpled from a heart attack and died.

He left behind him an astonishing legend of hard, deadly punching and ring cleverness. Decades went by in which aficionados argued over whether Benny Leonard or Joe Gans was the greatest pound-for-pound fighter of all time. Even the appearance of great warriors such as Henry Armstrong and Ike Williams did not change the nature of this debate. Only in recent times has it been altered by the appearance of Roberto Duran and Julio Cesar Chavez.

Whatever the upshot of the debate, it cannot be denied that Benny Leonard, like Joe Gans, was a ring marvel, who will be revered as long as there is reverence for the supreme practitioners of the Noble Art.

NOTE TO CHAPTER SIX

BENNY LEONARD
  Lightweight champion of the world: 1917–25.
  Total Bouts. 210.
  Won: 89 (71 by KO; 18 by decision).
  Lost: 5 (4 by KO; 0 by decision; 1 by foul).
  Draws: 1.
  No Decision: 115.

7

Tales of the Forgotten

Benny Leonard was a tough act to follow. In the eyes of fight fans, those who tried did not succeed. On Leonard's retirement in 1925, the New York Commission set up a tournament to determine his successor. The title was won on 13 July 1925 at Long Island City, New York, when Jimmy Goodrich of Scranton, Pennsylvania, stopped Stanislaus Loazya of Chile in the second round. Goodrich was tough and worthy but otherwise undistinguished. He won forty-four fights in his career, 1923–30 – and lost thirty-three. His reign didn't last long. On 7 December of the same year, he was trounced on points over fifteen rounds at the Broadway Auditorium, Buffalo, New York, by veteran Rocky Kansas.

Kansas, a native of Buffalo, had been in the ring for fifteen years prior to winning the crown. He had lost twice to Benny Leonard. Although Rocky was durable and packed a powerful wallop in either hand, he brought no especial distinction to the lightweight championship. On 3 July 1926, he faced clever challenger Sammy Mandell, at Comiskey Park, Chicago. The State of Illinois, which had banned boxing after the McGovern–Gans scandal, had now allowed it back provided that no contests exceeded ten rounds. Mandell outboxed Kansas easily to take the title.

Sammy was in fact a good boxer who could punch with authority. His trainer was the legendary bantamweight, Jack Blackburn, who went on to train the immortal Joe Louis. He had been trading punches since 1920. His boxing skills were impressive. Sportswriter J J Johnston recalled seeing him in action at Kid Howard's Gym, State Street, Chicago. After making a fool out of some mediocre sparring partner, Mandell faced a heavyweight, Captain Bob Roper, who was built like a bull and was regarded as a legitimate challenger to the heavyweight crown then worn by Gene Tunney. Johnston wrote:

What happened in the next three minutes was almost unbelievable. I was there. I saw it, but to this day my senses seem blurred, as Roper's must have been at Mandell's speed. About midway in the round Capt. Bob got Sammy in a corner, and for a brief second it seemed that this Goliath v David encounter would end in tragedy. Roper was steaming at his inability to lay a glove on Mandell, and the guffaws coming from the crowd probed a nerve center making his frustration worse. Don't know how, but while Bob was punching holes in the air, Sammy ducked under and was around the big man. Then, in one quick move, he planted his foot on the seat of Roper's trunks in a playful gesture.

Two former greats, lightweight Battling Nelson and heavyweight Jack Johnson were there to watch that exhibition. They were good friends who enjoyed cordial arguments. 'No one since Joe Gans could have done what

Mandell just did,' said Johnson. For once, Nelson agreed with him.

Mandell's record was good. He twice beat Jackie Fields, world welterweight champion 1929–30 and 1932–3. Phil McGraw, Luis Vincentini, and the outstanding Sid Terris were other victims. On 21 May 1928, the champion put his crown on the line against the great future champion, Jimmy McLarnin. Nat Fleischer declared that Mandell 'uncovered one of the finest exhibitions ever seen in New York' as he slipped and slid to an unarguable fifteen-round decision. It says something for the state of the lightweight division that McLarnin received $50,000 and Mandell $75,000.

'He gave me a beautiful boxing lesson,' McLarnin told Peter Heller many years later. 'He was a great boxer. I didn't defeat him, although I boxed him twice after that and did better. But the first time he defeated me in a fifteen-round fight. My first fifteen-round fight. The very first thing he did was stick his thumb in my eye, which isn't cricket.'

The 1929 National Boxing Consensus of the lightweight division as reported by Wilbur Wood of the New York *Sun* had seventy-two out of seventy-five boxing experts voting Mandell as Number One on merit with a .996%. The great future champion, Tony Canzoneri, was voted second at .852. A match was made. Mandell was confident and he had his supporters. The National Consensus of 1926 had had him second to Sid Terris, a man he would later beat. 1927 and 1928 had seen fifty-nine out of sixty experts choosing Mandell as the best in the division.

On 2 August 1929, Mandell fought the great Tony Canzoneri, who had recently lost the world featherweight championship. This was an all-action contest. 'Sammy was sharp that night,' Nat Fleischer observed as the champion took an undisputed ten-round decision. The next challenger, after two startlingly good performances by Mandell against recognized all-time greats, was unheralded Al Singer, Yankee Stadium, New York, 17 July 1930. Sammy had reigned for four years and few gave Singer a dog's chance. The crowd was astounded when Singer flattened Mandell for the count at 1.46 of the first round. Perhaps Singer's mentor, Benny Leonard, had something to do with it.

Mandell boxed on until 1934. Meanwhile Singer signed to face Tony Canzoneri in the latter's second go at the lightweight crown, Madison Square Garden, New York, 14 November 1930. This was the fourth fastest knockout in championship history. Canzoneri bulled Singer into his corner and ripped into him with fast combinations that sent him flying through the ropes to squat helplessly on the ring apron as he was counted out at 1.06 of the first round. Afterwards he was helped to his feet by Canzoneri's manager, Sam Goldman. Singer has the dubious distinction of being the only boxer to have won and lost his crown by one-round knockouts.

The Twenties were well and truly over. There were new times coming. People would suffer during the Great Depression but the ethnic wars would bring renewed days of glory to the division.

NOTE TO CHAPTER SEVEN

JIMMY GOODRICH
    Lightweight champion of the world: 1925
    Total bouts: 114.
    Won: 46 (6 by KO; 38 by decision; 2 by foul).
    Lost: 34 (1 by KO; 33 by decision).
    Draws: 15.
    No Decision: 19.

ROCKY KANSAS
Lightweight champion of the world: 1925–6.
Total bouts: 164.
Won: 64 (32 by KO; 32 by decision).
Lost: 12 (2 by KO; 8 by decision; 2 by foul).
Draws: 7.
No Decision: 81.

SAMMY MANDELL
Lightweight champion of the world: 1926–30
Total bouts: 168.
Won: 82 (28 by KO; 53 by decision; 1 by foul).
Lost: 17 (5 by KO; 11 by decision; 1 by foul).
Draws: 8.
No Decision: 61.
No Contest: 1.

AL SINGER
Lightweight champion of the world: 1930.
Total bouts: 70.
Won: 60 (24 by KO; 34 by decision; 2 by foul).
Lost: 8 (4 by KO; 4 by decision).
Draws: 2.

8

Ethnic Wars

The Wall Street Crash of 1929 and the ensuing Great Depression changed the nature of the fight game. The golden days were over. For example, heavyweight Jack Sharkey, champion of the world 1932–3, had been paid $300,000 for a non-title fight against Jack Dempsey in 1927 but received just $30,000 in 1936 for a non-title contest with Joe Louis. The millions of unemployed who stood waiting miserably in long lines for free bread and soup needed fighting heroes to make them feel better. Unfortunately, the heavyweight division was hardly inspiring, 1930–7, until Joe Louis took command. However, it was a wonderful period for the lightweight division.

'Into boxing's vacuum of emotional monotony, three men stood taller, much taller, than their respective heights of 5′ 4′′, 5′ 5½′′ and 5′ 7′′: Tony Canzoneri, Jimmy McLarnin and Barney Ross,' Bert R Sugar has rightly declared.

'They were the tonic the sport of boxing needed. And they were the heroes the fight fan needed.' Canzoneri was Italian, McLarnin was Irish and Ross was Jewish. Other outstanding heroes at the time included 'The Fargo Express', fierce Billy Petrolle from North Dakota who was rumoured to have Native American blood; Jackie 'Kid' Berg, the Anglo-Jewish pride of the East End of London; and Kid Chocolate of Cuba, who was black. Promoters saw financial opportunities in these ethnic wars whereby the fans cheered for their own.

Italian-American Tony Canzoneri, who had won the crown in 1930, 'rates with Joe Gans, Benny Leonard and Roberto Duran as one of the greatest lightweights ever in the ring', Bert Sugar states. The late old timer, Nat Fleischer, did not disagree with this opinion. 'Canzoneri was a real fighting champion, a colorful pugilist and a good crowd-pleaser,' he wrote. 'He could box well and could hit.'

This two-fisted, non-stop puncher had been born on 6 November 1908 in Slidell, Louisiana, though his family then moved to Brooklyn, New York. He turned professional boxer in 1925 and three years later, at the tender age of nineteen, he decisioned Benny Bass to become featherweight champion of the world. A skilful Frenchman, André Routis, outpointed Canzoneri over fifteen rounds to take this title, 28 September 1928. Canzoneri could be outboxed by a skilful man strong enough to take his punches, which is why it is unlikely he would have beaten Gans or Leonard; but he could no longer make the weight and stay fighting fit against an inferior opponent and this weakened him and slowed him down.

Beefing up to lightweight, he was outpointed by clever Sammy Mandell in his title challenge, as we have seen, but he then clocked Al Singer in one round to seize the crown. 1931 was quite a year for Canzoneri. He fought the great Kid Chocolate. This man had been born Eligio Sardinas in Cerro, Cuba, 6 January 1910. He had come to be managed by Luis Guitierrez, sports editor of Havana's *La Noche*, who trained him by making him watch old fight films, then taking him to the gym to practise all the moves he had seen. This method worked, for as an amateur, Kid Chocolate clocked up one hundred straight wins, with eighty-six by knockout. On entering the professional ranks, his boxing skill and punching power gave him another string of knockouts and he impressed hardened New Yorkers on his arrival in America, 1928. No black battler had attracted such admiration since the days of Joe Gans, Joe Walcott and Jack Johnson. 'Kid Chocolate, the Cuban bonbon, was a truly finished ringman,' Nat Fleischer stated. Bert Sugar agreed: 'Chocolate was one of boxing's greatest.'

Until 1930, he looked unbeatable. Then he started to lose his form. He dropped decisions to England's great Jackie 'Kid' Berg; to former world flyweight champion, Fidel LaBarba, whom he had defeated before; and, in a challenge for the world featherweight championship, to Battling Battalino. Unfortunately he had caught syphilis and this was affecting his performances. Amazingly enough, though, this did not stop him from winning the world junior lightweight crown from Benny Bass on 15 July 1931. On 20 November 1931, he challenged Tony Canzoneri for the world lightweight championship. Canzoneri spoiled Kid Chocolate's style with non-stop body punching, slowing down his superior speed, to win the fifteen-round decision.

Nevertheless, this fair defeat did not prevent Kid Chocolate from wearing the world junior lightweight crown until 1933, when Frankie Klick knocked him out in seven rounds in Philadelphia; and from knocking out Lew Feldman on 13 October 1932 to earn New York recognition as world featherweight champion, relinquishing his claim in 1933 because he could no longer make the weight. Instead, the man Nat Fleischer called 'an excellent boxer, with an abundance of ring skill and a good puncher', once again challenged Tony Canzoneri. This time he was not assisted by rapidly fading health and Canzoneri knocked him out in the second round. It was all downhill after that, although we should not forget that in 161 bouts from 1928 to 1938, he won 145, with sixty-four knockouts.

The fact that Tony Canzoneri was twice able to take the measure of Kid Chocolate says much for his fighting qualities. On 24 April 1931, he had fought England's Jackie 'Kid' Berg in Brooklyn, New York, in a match whereby both men agreed to put Canzoneri's lightweight crown and Berg's world junior welterweight crown on the line. Berg was the greatest fighter that London's East End had produced since the days of the immortal Ted 'Kid' Lewis. Like Lewis, he specialized in swarming all over his American opponents and beating them at their own game. However, this did not work with the ferociously busy and active Canzoneri, who flattened Berg in the third.

On 23 June 1933, Italian hero Canzoneri put both his titles on the line against Jewish hero, Barney Ross. Ross, born Beryl David Rosofsky, outboxed Tony to take his titles, making it clear why he had lost only one of his forty-eight fights. Showing that this was no fluke, Ross gave Canzoneri a return and did it again on 12 September 1933. Their first fight had been scheduled for ten rounds. This one went fifteen and Ross was awarded a split decision. One and all agreed that these were terrific contests. Nat Fleischer called them 'sizzling'.

Canzoneri showed his inner strength by coming back strongly. On 10 May 1935, after the undefeated Ross had given up his title to pursue his quest for the welterweight crown, Tony met rugged Lou Ambers for the lightweight championship. 'He beat me the first time,' Ambers admitted. 'I was nervous. He was my idol. I liked him the best and suddenly I'm in the ring with him, fighting him. That's the first time I fought for the title. I didn't do what I should have done.' Having become the first boxer ever to regain the lightweight championship, Canzoneri promptly offered Ambers a return match, 3 September 1936. 'I was thankful,' Ambers told Peter Heller. 'I says okay. We fought again and I won the title. When I fought him the second time then I beat him, a year after. I was a tough son of a gun.' Ambers was awarded the fifteen-round decision.

Tony kept going. On 8 May 1936 he faced Irish hero and legendary Champion Jimmy McLarnin in a non-title bout. He might have lost his title but he had not lost his dignity. This fight, in New York's legendary Madison Square Garden, did not start well for Canzoneri. After the referee's instructions, he walked right into the hanging ring microphone and sustained a cut that would later require twelve stitches. Unsurprisingly, McLarnin won the first round easily: yet Canzoneri came back to take the play away from his formidable foe, flooring him in the second round and then outpunching him to take the ten-round decision. They met again in the same venue five months later on 5 October 1936. This time McLarnin cut Canzoneri badly over his right eye and took advantage of that to win the ten-round decision.

No one ever knocked out Canzoneri until the fateful night of 1 November 1938, when he fought Brooklyn's Al 'Bummy' Davis, one of the most savage and dirty fighters who ever lived. Canzoneri was past his prime and, for the first time in his life, the count of ten was tolled over him when he fell from Davis's wicked left hook in the third round. 'The crowd booed Davis,' Bert Sugar commented, 'because Tony Canzoneri had been a great champion and the fans loved him until the end.' Wisely, he hung up his gloves. Then he entered show business, doing a night club act with comedian Joey Adams. 'He played the boxing buffoon, but the laughs he brought were honestly come by,' Gene Ward wrote. 'He had the wonderful gift of looking back and laughing at himself, and making others laugh with him.'

Canzoneri had won eight titles in the course of his remarkable career. A ninth, the world bantamweight championship, had only been denied him by Bud Taylor in a terrific ten-round draw. 'All of Canzoneri's fights were furious,' was Gene Ward's verdict. 'Tony was no slickster. He fought with the ferocity of the backwater bayous, where the weak were sucked in beneath the black waters ... he never failed to please the crowd.' Pete Herman, the great world bantamweight champion 1917–20 and 1921 had told Canzoneri: 'You will be a great fighter, my boy, because you have a great heart.' Tony always gave his all and that was why the people loved him; not just the Italians. Unfortunately, at the comparatively early age of fifty-one, his great heart finally gave out on 9 December 1959 at the Hotel Bryant, just off Broadway at 54th Street, Manhattan. Gene Ward's 'Requiem for a Lighter Weight' is appropriate, though sad:

> Police found a gold watch in the room. It was given to Canzoneri by the Boxing Writers Association in 1955. 'To a great fellow', it was inscribed. Also found were a number of photographs of the former champ in his ring attire and of his daughter and ex-wife. There was also $22.21.

His old antagonist, Jimmy McLarnin, with whom Canzoneri swopped decisions, did not end his days so sadly. The man the fans called 'Baby Face' was born on 17 December 1907 in Belfast, Northern Ireland, then grew up in Canada. Moving to California to begin his professional boxing career in 1923, he soon became the hero of the Irish by winning his first thirty-one bouts and beating future world flyweight champion, Fidel LaBarba. 'I fought McLarnin my second, my third, and my fifth professional fight,' LaBarba later told Peter Heller. 'McLarnin was an experienced fighter ... When the fight was over, I thought I won ... The referee turned around, he says, "Fuck LaBarba!" ' They fought again. 'It ended up, according to the slips, a draw,' LaBarba said. 'So then they said we're going to have another fight eventually. It was a close fight. I don't know whether I won or not, but he got the decision, and probably rightly so. We've always been the best of friends. I speak the highest praise of him. He was a hell of a fighter.'

McLarnin reminisced:

When I first came to California I was very small – 4 ft 11 in – and weighed 108 pounds ... When I fought Fidel LaBarba he was a flyweight and I was a bantamweight. I was sixteen years old at the time. Fidel was rough. He was one of the best left hookers. He was strong and I could move good. I was a good boxer. I had a long reach, so I used it. I kept jabbing and running, jabbing and running. And I really ran, I don't mind telling you, because it's a very silly pair of feet that stay around and let your face get punched. So I kept moving and kept my left jab right in his face. He had a great left hook to the stomach. Oh, boy, he hit me a few times and I thought all my teeth were being pulled out. He was a puncher.

McLarnin probably fought more past, present and future world champions than any other man in boxing history, defeating thirteen of them during his astonishing career. He was fortunate in being managed by the cantankerous but fiercely protective 'Pop' Foster. 1925 saw him defeat the great world flyweight champion, Pancho Villa, in a non-title bout. He lost to future world bantamweight champion, Bud Taylor, beat him on a foul, then dropped a decision to him in early 1926. He had ended 1925 by knocking out future world welterweight champion, Jackie Fields, in two rounds. McLarnin recalled:

Pancho Villa ... I think Pancho underrated me. I had a good jab and could box good ... It was a tough fight. On the inside he kept hitting me on the ears. He was a great infighter. I wound up with two black ears ... He was a great little fighter. Jackie Fields was a real great champ. I fought him as a featherweight ... I believe he had trouble making weight for me. I caught him early, second round. I just happened to get lucky.

Fields, too, had his memories:

I was a kid seventeen years old. He knocked me out and broke my jaw and I quit fighting ... Taking weight off, that was my lesson ... The first round I outboxed him. The second round I remember just like it was yesterday. I walked out there, started to throw my left jab, and the next thing I knew I was on the floor and the guy was counting ... (When I got up) I thought I had my hands up and it looked like he was coming to me in slow motion. The next thing I knew I was on the floor again. And I got up. Well, he knocked me down five times and they threw the towel in. I was very disheartened. My jaw was this big ... And when I came home my mother beat the shit out of me for being a fighter. You know how Jewish mothers are ...

McLarnin hardly had this problem when he iced former world featherweight champion, Louis 'Kid' Kaplan, in eight rounds, 18 October, 1927. The best account of this fight is surely that of McLarnin himself:

But I was fooled. He come charging out and the first punch he hit me knocked me down. I'd never been knocked down before. When I get up, he knocks me down again. I'm like a yo-yo. He keeps knocking me down, and my jaw is sore. Then I find out the first punch he hit me broke my jaw, and I'm in terrible shape. He keeps knocking me down and I keep getting up. And, all of a sudden, I notice after the fourth round that Kaplan's getting awful tired from hitting me. So Pop says, 'When he starts that hook move in.' So I'm waiting and I move in and hit him with a right hand and down goes Kaplan. Boy, do I get confidence! So I start knocking Kaplan down. I knocked him down about ten times and I'm getting so arm-weary, so we're both exhausted, especially me. Pop says, 'Go get him before he gets out of that corner,' so I walked out and bang, I hit him with a right hand and down he goes, and that was it. That got me into New York.

This was an under-statement. 'Combining the looks of an angel and the kick of a mule, he had become boxing's biggest drawing card since Jack Dempsey retired,' Bert Sugar states. He was matched with 'the uncrowned champion', outstanding Jewish fighter, Sid Terris – a fight best described by Sam Taub on radio:

> Terris comes out fast at the opening gong ... Terris jabs McLarnin and gets away ... Sid leaps in with two more straight lefts ... Terris is boxing beautifully tonight ... McLarnin has not started a punch yet ... Sid is in again with that straight left ... He's fast as lightning ... Terris leads again ... *Oi! Oi! Oi!* ... Terris is down ... McLarnin nailed him with a right to the chin ... There's the count ... Seven ... Eight ... Nine ... Ten ... *Oi!* ... *Oi!* ... *Oi!* ... It's all over! ... Terris is knocked out ...

McLarnin followed up this victory by beating the best Jewish fighters that New York had to offer; and this at a time when these exquisite boxers ruled the lower divisions. Joe Glick, Joey Sangor, Ruby Goldstein, Sergeant Sammy Baker and one-time lightweight champion Al Singer were all taken into camp. Not that Jewish fighters were his only victims: McLarnin lost a fifteen-round decision to world lightweight champion Sammy Mandell in 1928, though he defeated him in a non-title fight in 1929 and again a year later. Leading contender Ray Miller stopped McLarnin for the only time in his ring career in 1928 but was soundly beaten in a return match. In 1930, McLarnin defeated future world welterweight champion, Young Jack Thompson: then he faced 'The Fargo Express', Billy Petrolle.

Petrolle had 157 fights from 1910–34, winning eighty-five

with sixty-three knockouts. Nat Fleischer called this one McLarnin's 'most thrilling bout'. Billy Petrolle was still a legend when Joseph Heller wrote his great novel, *Catch-22* and followed it with a short story in which the military commanding officer is always shouting at the men that they must accomplish their tasks 'or you'll never be able to go fifteen rounds with Billy Petrolle'. In Fleischer's words:

> McLarnin took a licking that might have spelled finis to the career of a less courageous, stout-hearted battler. No one who saw that mill in the Garden in 1930 can ever forget it. Dropped in the opening round with a jaw-smash that hit him with the force of a club, Jimmy got to his feet and from then to the finish absorbed terrific punishment, yet refused to quit even when asked to do so by Referee Patsy Haley.

Yes, he did go fifteen rounds with Billy Petrolle and avenged the defeat with two subsequent victories.

There were mixed fortunes for McLarnin in 1932. He lost a decision to former welterweight and future middleweight champion, Lou Brouillard: but he did stop all-time great Benny Leonard. McLarnin admitted this victory gave him scant pleasure:

> Benny Leonard was my idol when I was young. He must have been one of the great fighters of all time. He was a pretty fat man when he fought me. He watched me train, and I had a bad habit of leaning under a right hand, and the very first punch that he hit me, I saw a million stars. He'd been watching me for quite awhile. I made a mistake, and you can't make mistakes with him. If he'd been a little young … I shook it off, come out of it, and finally knocked him out in seven rounds. But he was a tough old cookie, even at that age.

By this time, sportswriters were hailing McLarnin as being the greatest pound-for-pound fighter of his era. Certainly, he was the greatest lightweight who never wore the crown. On 29 May 1933 he beefed up to welterweight to challenge Young Corbett III for the championship. Corbett was no pushover. His record shows victories over the great welterweight and middleweight champion, Mickey Walker, as well as the great future light-heavyweight champion, Billy Conn, who would give Joe Louis so much trouble. Said McLarnin:

Corbett was a great fighter. He was unlucky. I was fortunate. We both threw punches at the same time and I happened to hit first. He was coming in on my punch, and I just hit first with the most. First round. It didn't last long. Two minutes. You try for years and years and years. You struggle and you get to the top of your profession. I imagine it's the same in any kind of endeavour and I was thrilled, no kidding about it. It was probably the happiest night of my fight career.

'With his appearance in the field,' wrote an approving Nat Fleischer, 'the division received a lift. It began to thrive again, with large gates and huge attendances once more making the class an outstanding one in popularity.' Jewish Barney Ross gave up the lightweight crown to challenge McLarnin in three classic contests, winning the first, losing the second but winning the third. The first contest alone resulted in a paying live gate of $186,000, with $60,000 for McLarnin.

After winning, losing, regaining and then losing the world welterweight championship on points, McLarnin engaged in two contests with the great Tony Canzoneri, as we have seen. Both men 'fought like demons', according to eye-witness Nat Fleischer, with Canzoneri winning the first decision and McLarnin winning the return. McLarnin's last fight was a non-title match with world lightweight champion Lou Ambers, 'The Herkiner Hurricane', on 20 November 1936 in

New York. 'I won and didn't get hurt ...' McLarnin said.
'... I gave Ambers quite a beating, a real bad beating.' At that
point, McLarnin quit as a winner and hung up his gloves. He
had won sixty-three of seventy-seven contests, with twenty by
knockout, drawn three, and lost eleven against the best men
at his weight in the world, with just one defeat by KO.
Subsequently he founded a prosperous tool-and-dye business,
organizing a sales branch to represent firms as late as 1970. He
became a friend of Bing Crosby, with whom he played golf.
His wife Lillian gave him a son and three daughters, resulting
in grandchildren. McLarnin and wife retired to a luxurious
home in Glendale, Los Angeles, California.

Barney Ross was the man who rescued New York Jewish
pride from the fearful pasting it had been given fairly and
squarely by Jimmy McLarnin. Born the son of a rabbi on
New York's tough Lower East Side, 23 December 1909, Ross
soon moved with his family to Chicago. After a respectable
career as an amateur boxer, he turned professional in 1929.
'Barney was a superb boxer with great speed who could take
punishment with the best of them,' Bert Sugar wrote, adding,
'He was never knocked out – or even down – in eighty-one pro
contests.' As noted, the Jewish hero decisioned the Italian
hero for the world lightweight and junior welterweight titles
in a grand contest on 23 June 1933. Ross then gave up the
lightweight crown to go after McLarnin at welterweight.

A tremendous match took place in Long Island City's
Madison Square Garden Bowl, New York, 28 May 1934.
Previously regarded as a cautious, skilful boxer, Ross threw
caution to the winds and came out fighting, wading right into
hard-fisted McLarnin to slug it out with him. 'But I was
having hand trouble ...' McLarnin stated years after the
event, continuing, 'Barney wasn't a great puncher, but he was
a terrific boxer, he could take a good punch, and he was smart.
Especially in the last ten seconds he'd always finish with a big
flurry.' Ross floored McLarnin in the ninth and walked away
with a split decision and the title.

There had to be a return and this took place on 17 September 1934, Long Island, New York. 'Barney was a well-conditioned boy ...' said McLarnin. 'I was anxious to fight him again.' This was hardly surprising in view of the total of 90,344 fans who paid a total of $473,712 to see their three great fights. This time McLarnin won by split decision and regained his kingdom. Three wins gave Ross the right to a rematch with McLarnin on 28 May 1935 in New York's Polo Grounds. Nat Fleischer called this one 'a thrilling exhibition of ring cleverness combined with sharp hits'. 'And there was one thing about Barney,' said McLarnin, 'he couldn't hurt you too bad. He wasn't a great puncher but he could stab you pretty good, make you look like a nickel, very embarrassing. But he was quite an attraction. The Jewish and the Irish in New York together were good attractions.' After fifteen rounds of all-out action, with neither man backing off, the fighters embraced. The decision and the championship went back to Ross.

Ross ruled the welterweight division for three years. Nat Fleischer called his performances 'scintillating' and declared: 'The best of all training camps were Barney Ross's at Grossinger's, a summer resort in New York's Catskill Mountains. Besides the serious training routine, there was always time for fun ...' Ross won against Ceferino Garcia, future world middleweight champion, and also beat him twice in non-title matches. He also defended his title ably against accomplished Izzy Janazzo. On 31 May 1938, he put his championship on the line against future world lightweight champion, black Henry Armstrong, who was at that time also the featherweight king. Armstrong, then at his peak and an all-time great, gave Ross a frightful beating. As Armstrong later stated:

And I beat Barney Ross so on that night, it was terrific. I carried him the last four rounds ... He wanted to last on his feet ... I was ready to knock him out because I had him cut up ... He was bleeding, blood was on me from him, and my gloves was just watered with blood. The ref was going to stop it and Barney fought with his corner men. They said, 'Barney, let us throw the towel in, we don't want to see you get hurt.' He says, 'If you throw the towel in I'll never speak to you again ...' I had just said, 'Pull this glove up, because I'm going to knock Barney out. I don't want to crucify him. I don't want to hurt him no more. He can't see now.' ... I got out there, about the eleventh round, I said, 'How you feel, Barney?' He said, 'I'm dead.' I said, 'Jab and run, and I'll make it look good.' He said, 'It's a deal, Hank.' And he just jabbed, bang, bang, bang. Then after the fight he said, 'You're the greatest,' and he just hugged me. They had to take him to the hospital. That was it. He was a dynamic guy, and he showed valor in Guadalcanal, too.

Here Armstrong was referring to the undoubted bravery of his opponent in the Second World War. For Ross, the undefeated lightweight and junior welterweight champion, who had won and lost the welterweight crown with dignity, hung up his gloves, then joined the United States Marines to serve his country. After receiving a sharpshooter's medal, he went on to earn the Congressional Medal of Honor for saving the lives of 10 US Marines trapped in a Guadalcanal foxhole by single-handedly killing twenty Japanese soldiers in a feat of astonishing wartime bravery. Unfortunately, Ross suffered war wounds and was prescribed morphine as a pain-killer; and he became addicted to it. After a grim period, he beat this addiction and it was later dramatized in the film, *Monkey on My Back*. Even so, his later years were not happy ones and on 17 January 1967, this brave and noble warrior died of cancer.

Canzoneri, Ross, McLarnin, Kid Chocolate, Kid Berg, Henry Armstrong and their many fine contemporaries did indeed battle for ethnic supremacy as the fight fans bayed for their own; and in 1936, the Italian-Americans were cheering their lightweight champion, Lou Ambers. Yet the innate nobility of these warriors should not be ignored. The first heavyweight champion of the world under Queensberry Rules, James J Corbett, used to visit Jimmy McLarnin in his dressing room. His words were: 'Jimmy, remember one thing. A fighter can always afford to be a gentleman.' 'And I've never forgotten that,' said McLarnin. Nor did the others of this era, whatever their race, religion, colour or creed.

NOTE TO CHAPTER EIGHT

TONY CANZONERI

Lightweight champion of the world: 1930–3; 1935–6.
Featherweight champion of the world: 1928.
World junior welterweight champion: 1931–2; 1933.
Total bouts: 176.
Won: 139 (44 by KO; 95 by decision).
Lost: 24 (1 by KO; 22 by decision; 1 by Foul).
Draws: 10.
No Decision: 3.

BARNEY ROSS

Lightweight champion of the world: 1933.
World junior welterweight champion: 1933.
Welterweight Champion of the World: 1934; 1935–8.
Total bouts: 81.
Won: 73 (22 by KO; 51 by decision).
Lost: 4 (0 by KO; 4 by decision).
Draws: 3.
No Decision: 1.

9

Hurricanes of Black and White

Sometimes in life, a man does not receive just credit for his achievements. An obvious example is Lou Ambers, the world lightweight champion in 1936. This man was defeated only eight times in 102 contests and he mixed it with all the best men of his time, yet his name is rarely mentioned when the ring's more illustrious luminaries are discussed. Perhaps posterity can remedy this undue neglect.

'The Herkimer Hurricane' was born Luigi D'Ambrosio, the fifth of ten children, in Herkimer, New York state. His father owned a saloon and a candy store in the locality but was driven out of business by the Depression. Lou Ambers started fighting to help out his family. He began with semi-amateur bouts at the age of sixteen in 1929, fighting in the rough clubs of upstate New York. Those were the days when the winner received between two and five dollars. At times the pickings were so lean that Ambers had to go to the local jailhouse and ask for a bed for the night. His purses improved to the princely sum of $7.00. His break came when a dazzling performance at Coney Island drew an ovation from the crowd and clever but unscrupulous manager, Al Weill, later to handle Rocky Marciano, spotted a winner and persuaded Ambers to turn professional.

'As a kid, I was a bad boy, to tell you the truth,' Ambers admitted as an old man. 'I had a lot of trouble. I'd fight with anybody.' This spirit stood him in good stead during his march through tough contenders at tougher New York fight clubs. He endeared himself to the crowds with his straight talk, his pleasant appearance, his aggressive but crafty fighting style and his ready and willing smile. In two years he lost only one decision in forty-eight fights and so qualified for a challenge against the great champion, Tony Canzoneri. As noted, Canzoneri gave the inexperienced youngster a hiding, though Lou went the fifteen-round distance.

Ambers came back on 1 July 1935 to meet future world welterweight champion, Polish Fritzie Zivic, a vicious, dangerous and dirty fighter. Ambers takes up the story:

In about the seventh round, he threw a right hand and I stepped back holding my mouth open. He hit me on the chin and broke my jaw. I went on with the fight just the same and I went to the corner and my manager says, 'What's the matter? What's the matter?' Blood was coming out of my mouth. He started to throw the towel in and I says, 'You don't throw nothing in. I'll fight him. I'm going to finish this fight.' So I went in and I beat him. For the next two rounds I beat the devil out of him. See, that's when you're in good shape. When you can go when something's wrong. I won the fight all right.

Lou went on to beat former junior welterweight champion,

Frankie Klick, conqueror of the legendary Kid Chocolate; former world featherweight champion, Alberto 'Babe' Arizmendi; and leading contender, Tony Scarpati. This contest ended in tears. Ambers decked Scarpati in the seventh and Scarpati did not get up again. He was taken to hospital, where he died three days later. 'It broke my heart,' said Ambers, who wanted to quit after that but was talked out of it by manager Al Weill. 'But every once in a while,' Ambers confessed, 'I'd look in that corner and I'd see like a picture of Tony Scarpati, God rest his soul.'

This tragedy did not stop Ambers from winning the lightweight championship off Tony Canzoneri in their return match, 3 September, 1936. The new champion's reign began ingloriously, however, when he received a non-title beating from Jimmy McLarnin a couple of months later. Nevertheless, Ambers redeemed himself with a successful title defence against Tony Canzoneri, beating him to the punch all night long. One judge gave him every single one of fifteen rounds.

The celebrated Carnival of Champions took place in New York on 23 September 1937 and lightweight champion Lou Ambers was top of the bill, with Puerto Rican Pedro Montanez as his challenger. They were in good company, as middleweights Fred Apostoli and Marcel Thil, welterweights Barney Ross and Ceferino Garcia and bantamweights Sixto Escobar and Harry Jeffra battled for supremacy; but accounts of the Ambers–Montanez contest are disturbingly varied. All agree that Montanez was a dangerous puncher. A year before, he had won an over-the-weight decision over Ambers, which had been booed so loudly and long that the next fight could not be introduced. Now Ambers received $83,000, the biggest purse of his career so far, to defend his title. John E Heany, one of Amber's greatest fans, called this bout 'one of his least luminous'. The great Benny Leonard was enigmatic in stating that Ambers 'gave a very clever performance. I think his handlers didn't do right in not sending him after Montanez, who was a total flop.' By contrast, Nat Fleischer declared that

'Ambers successfully and brilliantly defended his crown.' Unfortunately, there are no films known to the present writer which would enable an independent judgement. The plain fact is that the fight went fifteen rounds with Ambers the winner by split decision; the referee scored it a draw.

It would be more difficult, though, to score Ambers's next fight against 'Hurricane' Henry Armstrong, one of the most remarkable boxers who ever lived. The man also known as 'Homicide Hank' was born on 12 December 1912 in Columbus, Mississippi as Henry Jackson. His family moved to St Louis, Missouri, and endured all the vile prejudice of the time against black people. This was all the more absurd because, although Armstrong's grandmother had been a black slave, his grandfather had been a white plantation owner. His mother was half Cherokee Indian. Armstrong began his fighting career in the nauseating Battle Royals which were still being shamefully conducted in St Louis as late as 1929. Then he travelled anywhere, looking for fights in Montana, Nevada, Oregon and California, ready to fight anybody for a few bucks. It seemed as if times hadn't changed since the early days of the near-starving Joe Gans.

There was one important difference, though. Gans had been a master of boxing. Armstrong was an incredible fighter, willingly taking one to land five and never stopping his frontal assault, his fast and furious barrage of leather. His body was physically exceptional. 'A freak of a generation', one doctor subsequently declared in a medical report. 'He is so perfect a human dynamo that he is scarcely a fair opponent for any normal man near his weight. He must have an oversized heart, not to the point of pathological enlargement, but above normal. His pulse beat of 59 compared with the normal 72 ... makes him capable of astonishing endurance...'

This did not prevent an inexperienced Armstrong from being kayoed in his first professional bout in 1931 and he had a rough ride for the next two years. Baby Arizmendi, recognized 1934–5 as world featherweight champion on the

West Coast, beat Armstrong via decision in 1933, 1934 and
1935. Nevertheless, the fighting heart of Armstrong attracted
the attention of actors Eddie Mead and Al Jolson who bought
his contract from his crooked and exploitative manager Wirt
Ross for $10,000. George Raft also took a share in the deal.
The fact that Mead was connected to gangsters such as Owney
Madden, Bugsy Siegel and Frankie Carbo might have been
regrettable but it gave Armstrong the big breaks he needed.

He defeated Arizmendi in their fourth fight, 1936. After
that he knocked out future NBA world lightweight champion,
Juan Zurita. In a non-title fight, he decisioned the world
featherweight champion recognized by the New York
Commission, Mike Belloise, and stopped him in four rounds a
year later. Junior lightweight champion Frankie Klick, who
had beaten Kid Chocolate, was stopped in a non-title contest
by Armstrong who went on to overwhelm former world
featherweight champion Benny Bass.

These well-earned victories gave Armstrong a title shot at
last against reigning featherweight king Petey Sarron in
Madison Square Garden, New York, 29 October 1937.
Armstrong won the crown with a ferocious sixth round
knockout. This was the climax to an incredible string of
twenty-six knockouts in twenty-seven victories during that
glorious year.

1938 saw him flatten future world featherweight champion,
Chalky Wright, and gain another decision over Baby
Arizmendi. Mead, Jolson and Raft now looked for further
ways of making money out of their human dynamo. The
dreadful prejudice against black fighters which had been
exacerbated during the insolent reign of the great heavyweight
Jack Johnson, 1908–15, was still in evidence, but at least
Armstrong held the featherweight championship: and a black
phenomenon, Joe Louis, had just won the heavyweight crown
to become the most sensational box-office attraction since the
days of Jack Dempsey. Armstrong's management decided to
rival Joe Louis in pursuing a goal that had never been

achieved before. It was to go after three world championships and hold them all simultaneously – an idea straight out of Hollywood.

When negotiations with champion Lou Ambers at lightweight, Armstrong's natural build, were stalled by Lou's manager Al Weill, a match was made with welterweight champion, Barney Ross. Armstrong had to beef up from 126 to 147 pounds. He was fed on copious quantities of steak, potatoes and sweets. A day before the weigh-in, he had to drink huge quantities of water.

'Boy, about eleven o'clock you could hear the water every time I walked. Glug, glug, glug,' Armstrong later recalled. Ross was favoured to win at 3–1. As we have seen, Armstrong gave Ross such a pasting that Ross never fought again. Now it was time to fight Lou Ambers at lightweight to decide the issue between the 'Herkimer Hurricane' and 'Hurricane Hank'. Madison Square Garden was packed out on 17 August 1938.

This was 'one of the best fought in years,' Nat Fleischer wrote enthusiastically. ' ... blood-spattered battle ... "Hammerin" Hank was busy every second of the bout, swinging from all angles and taking advantage of split-second openings to put over a crushing blow ... When it seemed like Ambers was weakening, Lou would lash back with solid smashes that rocked Henry. There wasn't a second's rest for either man throughout the battle ... ' James F Dawson of *The New York Times* praised 'fifteen rounds of as fast, furious and savage fighting as has ever been seen here'. Ambers was floored in the fifth and sixth rounds but came back strongly. 'I fought him good and it was a good fight, tough fight,' Lou Ambers said. 'He was always coming in, but I was in good shape. I cut him in his mouth, cut the eye.' According to Armstrong:

That was the bloodiest fight I ever had in my life. Donovan (the referee) came over, I think it was the twelfth or thirteenth round, and said he was going to stop the fight. I asked him why, and he said, 'Look at the ring. It's full of blood.' I said, 'So what?' He said, 'It's your blood.' I said, 'Well, I'm not going to bleed no more.' He said, 'If you got that much damn nerve, I'll let you continue ... If you spit any more blood on this floor, I'm going to stop this fight.' ... Bingo, the bell rings. Thirteenth. Fourteenth. I finished those two rounds. Then I was getting weak because of my blood and then I started to swallow it. I could hear my stomach – rummmpp, ruummpp. This had to be in the fifteenth. I looked up and the Garden just completely blacked out.

Afterwards Armstrong asked, 'What did he hit me with?' 'He hit you with nothing,' his trainer told him, 'we had to take you off him. You almost knocked Ambers out!'

The result was a split decision in favour of the challenger, Henry Armstrong, who was awarded the lightweight championship of the World. He needed nine stitches in his lower lip. According to *The New York Times*, the verdict was greeted with 'a terrific din of jeers, boos and catcalls'. According to Nat Fleischer, although Ambers had left Armstrong looking 'wobbly and gory at the close of a vicious encounter', Armstrong was nevertheless 'the decisive winner'. The fairest verdict is surely that of Lou Ambers: 'He beat me out. Like I've always said, he was the better man than I was on that night.'

Armstrong's amazing feat of holding three undisputed world championships simultaneously will never be repeated. This was because Boxing Commissions started passing regulations which stated that a fighter could only hold one world title at a time. Meanwhile the triple champion defended his welterweight title successfully against future world middleweight champion, Ceferino Garcia, famed for his deadly 'bolo punch', and won a fair fifteen-round decision, following this with another welterweight defence against Al Manfredo, whom he halted in three rounds. Difficulties of making weight then caused him to relinquish the featherweight title.

Lou Ambers was now on the comeback trail. Nine straight victories in twelve months gave him the inalienable right to a rematch with Armstrong with the latter's lightweight crown at stake. These warriors met again at Yankee Stadium, New York, 22 August 1938, with Armstrong coming off a recent second victory over his old nemesis, Baby Arizmendi, and the result was controversial. 'Great was the confusion and loud the squawks ...' Nat Fleischer commented. However, the fight itself was no disappointment. James F Dawson, once again reporting for *The New York Times*, called it 'one of the greatest lightweight struggles seen here in years'. Ambers closed Armstrong's right eye, damaged his left and gashed his mouth again, although Armstrong rallied. The defending champion's manager, Eddie Mead, claimed afterwards that Ambers had done these deeds with his thumbs. It is hard to see how Ambers could have put his thumb in Armstrong's mouth. For his part, Armstrong had five rounds deducted for low blows by respected referee, Arthur Donovan. Nat Fleischer declared that he saw no gouging or thumbing by Ambers but that the referee's deductions from Armstrong were 'for what he termed low hitting, an unusual procedure in any contest, especially a title bout ...' What did the boxers say?

'I beat him,' Armstrong claimed, 'and he'll tell you today that's the fight that killed him. I beat him bad. I beat him worse than I did in the first. I gave him a body beating, he's never gotten over that ... They say I fouled him five times, which was the biggest lie in the world...'

'I took the title back away from him,' Ambers stated. 'He was a tough guy to fight.'

Ambers regained the championship on a split decision. 'The title was decided not on competition but on fighting ethics,' James F Dawson pronounced. 'Ambers did the job of his career,' Nat Fleischer dissented. 'He was a fighting demon.' Henry Armstrong did not share his opinion. ' ... they were going to take those three titles away from me anyway. I heard that Mike Jacobs (the promoter) had got an ultimatum from the government that he was monopolizing the boxing game by letting a man hold more than one title.'

Obviously a rubber match was in order. Champion Ambers married his sweetheart Margaret, honeymooned in Hawaii and then signed to defend against Armstrong again, the bout to take place on 1 December. Armstrong claimed illness and had the match postponed. Ambers continued to train but Armstrong postponed it twice more before it was cancelled. A long while later, Mrs Margaret Ambers told reporter John E Heany that after the men had retired from the ring, Armstrong paid a friendly visit to her home and told her that he had staged the delays because he had not wanted to fight her husband again. Bert Sugar thinks that Armstrong's furious pace had already been giving him burn-out as early as the first Ambers contest. For his part, Ambers averred that Armstrong gave him his toughest fights, declaring, 'He wasn't smart enough, but he was good.'

Smart or no, burn-out or not, 'Hurricane Hank' came back to astound the welterweight division he still ruled, defending his title no less than a record nineteen times with sixteen KOs, which is yet to be surpassed. This included a victory over the exquisitely skilful British Empire champion, Ernie Roderick, via an undisputed fifteen-round decision. He endeavoured to add the middleweight title to his lustrous laurels on 11 March 1940 when he fought a man he had already beaten, recently crowned Ceferino Garcia. This fight, available on video, saw non-stop body punching and untidy scrapping with Armstrong having the edge. The present writer concurs with past ringside reporters and outraged spectators in deploring the decision, which was a draw. Garcia kept his crown and Armstrong was robbed of his chance to achieve yet another world record.

Ambers, meanwhile, showed equally that he had as much fight left in him as ever when he squared off against unbeaten Al 'Bummy' Davis in a non-title contest on 23 February 1940 in New York. Davis was a street thug outside the ring and in it. Ambers was outweighed by 8 pounds. Even so, the vicious assaults of Davis did not trouble Lou. James F Dawson reported that Ambers gave Davis such a severe hiding that 'the crowd ridiculed Davis'. Nat Fleischer stated: 'Ambers never displayed such brilliance.' Mrs Margaret Ambers later fondly recalled that 'Lou got telegrams from all over Brooklyn, thanking him for giving Davis such a smacking.'

In later years, Davis would disgrace himself by deliberately hitting Fritzie Zivic low nine times in succession and when the referee tried to intervene, Davis gave him a kicking. About the only redeeming feature one can find in the life of this thug was that he was fearlessly loyal to his friends. When a gang of gunmen held up a bar owned by a friend, an unarmed Davis tackled them. He knocked out one, but was shot. Despite this, he chased the four gangsters out on to the sidewalk. They riddled him with bullets and he died the way he lived.

After these superb performances, Lou Ambers was now finding it difficult to make the lightweight limit and it showed on the night that he defended his crown against tough, hard-punching Texan redneck, Lew Jenkins, New York, 10 May 1940. After an indifferent start to his professional career, Jenkins had won attention by racking up a series of eight startling consecutive knockouts over ranked contenders, but was nevertheless the underdog at 16–5. The challenger amazed the crowd in 'striking with deadly accuracy and the precision of a rattlesnake', as Nat Fleischer put it. The iron-chinned Ambers was sent spinning to the canvas four times. Referee Billy Cavanagh rightly halted this one-sided affair in the third round. It was the first time that Lou had ever been stopped. *The Ring* stated that the strain of making the weight had left Ambers 'a dried-up human being, peaked and drawn'. 'I couldn't make the weight the first fight,' said Ambers: 'I just made it barely. When a fellow gets older in the game, you're going to weaken.' The return match was a lengthier repeat of the same story, New York, 28 February 1941. Ambers's manager, Al Weill, threw in the towel in the seventh round. ' ... To tell you the truth, honest to God, I seen the right hand come right to my face,' Ambers admitted. 'Now, I've always just stepped aside. That night I couldn't move. I'm stunned there. I got hit. He knocked me down. I got up. The same thing happened the second time.'

Ambers wisely chose to call it a day and hung up his gloves. Not so Armstrong, who was slogging on. Perhaps it was pride that caused him to tackle newly crowned Lew Jenkins, Ambers's conqueror, in a non-title contest. Jenkins cut his right eye badly that night of 17 July 1940 in New York but 'Hurricane Hank' stormed back to take the fight via sixth-round knockout.

On 4 October 1940 in New York, he defended his welterweight championship against mean Fritzie Zivic, a 6–1 underdog. By this time, the express train that was Armstrong had zoomed on so punishing a pace that it was running out of fuel. Zivic derailed it, astounding the sporting world by countering the champion with wicked uppercuts and cutting him over both eyes. 'He was just a nasty fighter, just a foul fighter,' said Armstrong. 'He did everything foul and, of course, when he got me, he got me when I was tired and I should have been resting but my manager wanted that money quick.'

Unsurprisingly, perhaps, Zivic's testimony is somewhat different:

> I don't think I won a point the first five rounds. He punched the shit out of me. I'm grabbing, ducking, blocking, he kept coming, he'd throw a left hook, bang! hit you right in the eye ... The first five rounds he beat me up more than the next twenty guys. I got mad. He hit me low, choked me, give me the elbow, and everything else ... I never complained ... I hit him low in the sixth round, I said, 'Pardon me.' I banged him again low, said,

'Pardon me.' ... The referee in the sixth round stopped the fight, looked at Armstrong, looked at me, and said, 'If you guys want to fight like this it's OK with me.' That's all I wanted to hear ... I busted him up, cut him here and cut him here ... When the eye was cut, I'd rub it with the laces to open it up a little more ... His mouth was cut real bad. He was too proud to spit the blood out. He swallowed it. Swallowing the blood made him sick ... He kept bleeding and bleeding ... It felt wonderful.

This charming young gentleman knocked Armstrong down in the final round and took his title on a unanimous fifteen-round decision.

There was no joy for Henry Armstrong in the return match, 17 January 1941, any more than there had been for Ambers in his second go against Jenkins. 'Homicide Hank' was beaten bloody and the fight had to be stopped in the twelfth. This was only Armstrong's second loss by KO over ten years of ferocious campaigning. He chose to emulate Ambers in retiring from the ring, but came back in the summer of 1942. Although he was slower than in his prime, he was still too much for most of the top contenders. He convincingly defeated future and ex-champs Juan Zurita (lightweight), Leo Rodak (featherweight) and repeated his win over Lew Jenkins. His victory over ex-champion Fritzie Zivic, his former conqueror, must have given him especial pleasure. 'I gave him a good beating,' Armstrong reminisced. 'I didn't try to knock him out. I just wanted to punish him.'

1943 started equally excitingly when Armstrong beat ex-lightweight champion Sammy Angott and halted the highly touted Tippy Larkin. This secured him a non-title match with Beau Jack, a tremendous fighter, recognized by New York as world lightweight champion. The contest took place in New York on 2 April 1943. According to Beau Jack:

The man I didn't want to box at all was my idol, Henry

Armstrong, but when he said, 'Beau, our friendship ceases when we go into the ring. We're friends on the outside, but when we go into the ring we're no more friends', so I told my manager I'll take the fight then. The greatest fighter that ever lived as far as I'm concerned. He's a fine man ... It's hard enough to win even one (title) and this one man got three. In your mind it come to you: *What must I do?* ... I was lucky enough to beat him, but if I had to go back over to fight him again, good as I loved to fight, I don't think that I'd want to do it. I don't think I'd want to go back over it again.

Beau Jack won the decision.

In the same year, Armstrong, the living legend of the present, climbed into the ring at Madison Square Garden, New York, to face the living legend of the future, Sugar Ray Robinson. Robinson is held by many experts to have been the greatest pound-for-pound pugilist who ever lived. He was welterweight champion 1946–51, retiring undefeated, and middleweight champion an incredible five times 1951–60. Armstrong allowed that 'Ray was clever' but declared:

It was a disgusting fight ... Ray just wouldn't fight. He told me he was going to run. I almost knocked him out in the third round. He'd always boasted that he'd never fight me. I was his idol. I said, 'Ray, this is the Garden and they're booing. I've never been booed in the Garden, so they must be booing you. Why don't you come on in and fight?' He said, 'The hell with you, Hank. I ain't going to get hit like that no more. If you can catch me, catch me. I'm going to try and win this fight on decision', and he just run. I couldn't get him. He won the fight. He won it on points.

That was the end of Armstrong's great days. Although he won sixteen out of nineteen fights in 1944, he lacked the old black magic and a loss to one Chester Slider convinced him finally that it was time to retire. The ensuing years saw him have a chequered career. He had earned a million dollars as triple champion. Who knows exactly where that money went? For example, Armstrong was paid $50,000 to defend his crown against Ernie Roderick in London but claimed he never received more than $15,000 from his management after 'deductions' and 'expenses'. 'We always used to call it the "bloodbath", the "swindle sheet",' he remarked indignantly. He changed management after Eddie Mead and Al Jolson, his previous managers, both died of heart attacks, though George Raft would live long and prosper, and claimed to have made a further $500,000 through his twenty-three-fight comeback, but nobody really knows where it all went, though one can guess. Certainly some losses were Armstrong's fault. He took to drinking more than was good for him and lost by his own estimation $15,000–20,000 on a badly scripted film about his life called *Keep Punching*, which was a failure at the box-office. He lost even more money on a West Coast nightclub. There was the taxman to pay, of course, for he had fallen into arrears; and the accountants and the lawyers. Times grew hard for Henry. He received a conditional discharge for brawling.

Fortunately, he came back, as he always had throughout his life. In 1951, he was ordained as a Baptist minister of the church and he proceeded to preach tough fighting and clean living. He returned to the place of his birth, St Louis, Missouri, where he became assistant pastor of the First Baptist Church and a director of the Herbert Hoover Boys' Club. By the age of sixty, he was living in modest comfort with his wife, beaming upon his married children and gaining extra pleasure and income through frequent journeys all over the United States to make personal appearances. His story has a happy ending.

So does that of Ambers. His marriage to Margaret lasted and they delighted in their three successful children. After serving in the Coast Guard during the Second World War,

Ambers settled in Phoenix, Arizona, and for a time worked for Reynolds Metal. Managers had taken much of his money too but he enjoyed his lot of modest comfort. There was talk of making a film about his life. His wife tells the story best: 'But after they talked with him, the writer said, "Lou, it's too clean. There's nothing that would rouse anybody up." Lou didn't drink, no dope, no gambling. Can you believe somebody's life is "too clean" for a movie? I thought, I thought, maybe that's what we need to give these kids – something that's too clean.'

'She's feisty, isn't she?' her husband said proudly. 'Oh, Jesus, I loved to fight,' he declaimed in another interview. 'If you try and try hard enough, you'll always succeed. But if you don't try, how the devil are you going to succeed?'

May these two great warriors now rest in peace.

NOTE TO CHAPTER NINE

LOU AMBERS
> Lightweight champion of the world: 1936–8: 1939–40.
> Total bouts: 102.
> Won: 88 (29 by KO; 59 by decision).
> Lost: 8 (2 by KO; 6 by decision).
> Draws: 6.

HENRY ARMSTRONG
> Lightweight champion of the world: 1938–9.
> Featherweight champion of the world: 1937–8.
> Welterweight champion of the world: 1938–40.
> Total bouts: 174.
> won: 145 (98 by KO; 47 by decision).
> Lost: 20 (2 by KO; 17 by decision; 1 by foul).
> Draws: 9.

10

The Good, the Bad
and the Ugly

The Second World War and America's entry after Japan's 1941 bombing of Pearl Harbor changed the world and obviously affected the less important sport of boxing. Champions Joe Louis (heavyweight), Gus Lesvenich (light-heavyweight), Tony Zale (middleweight), Freddie Cochrane (welterweight) and Willie Pep (featherweight) joined up with 12,000,000 Americans to march off to war against fascism. Their titles were properly frozen for the duration of the conflict.

One wonders why we do not find many lightweight champions to be serving in the armed forces at this time. Obviously they weren't being turned down by the recruiting sergeant because they had flat feet, sinus trouble or a bad case of backache. Low intelligence has never been a bar from joining the army, especially in wartime. How did fit, strong, alert men manage to avoid the unpleasant prospect of being maimed and/or killed?

A second pronounced effect upon the sport was the growing influence of organized crime. We have already seen how the great Henry Armstrong was horribly exploited in financial terms by his managers. Honour among thieves is a myth believed only by middle-class sentimentalists. These ruthless thugs and brutes and killers moved in on the fight game, spoiling its claims to be the Noble Art. Good, strong, honest men weren't there to prevent it: they were too busy risking their lives in defence of democracy.

It cannot be said, however, that Texan redneck, Lew Jenkins, world lightweight champion 1940–1, did not do his patriotic duty. He had three spells in the army. In later years he declared: 'In '39 and the first part of '40 I don't think there was ever a lightweight ever lived that could beat me, honest to God.' Most experts disagree, declaring Jenkins to have achieved greatness only in fleeting moments, but no one can deny that he rates highly among the ring's more colourful characters.

This man was born on 4 December 1916 in Texas, the son of migrant white farm workers. His fighting began on small town streets, moved on to touring carnival shows and was consolidated by his first stint in the US Army. His early professional record was nothing special. He had twenty-five fights in 1938, winning eighteen with twelve by KO, but losing five by decision with two KOs by Bobby Britton and Chino Alvarez. The following year saw him lose two decisions to Willie Joyce and he was KO'd by Pete Lello. After these setbacks he roared back to establish a winning streak of eight consecutive knockouts over the best men the division had to offer at the time. His victims included Primo Flores (twice), Billy Marquart and the man who used to be announced as 'the greatest that laid on a pair of gloves!' in Madison Square Garden, top contender Mike Belloise. He was a ferociously hard puncher with little subtlety. Either you nailed him or he nailed you. He relied on short, jolting hooks. His preparation for fights drove his trainers to despair.

'I quit smoking for two or three weeks,' Jenkins reminisced about the Belloise match, '... but I smoked all my life and that was the hardest thing in me, smoking ... I got drunk before the fight for a few days ...' Four more knockouts after Belloise, including one over highly rated future junior welterweight champion Tippy Larkin in just a round and a one-round knockout revenge over his former conqueror, Chino Alvarez, brought Lew Jenkins his title shot against Lou Ambers. 'I trained very good,' Jenkins said, 'but a week before the fight, I broke all the rules ... All the rules you could break, I broke. Screwing, the whole goddamn thing ... I was never in shape in my life, never in condition. I'd go out and run a little bit and sit down, smoke a cigarette, rest for a while. I had bottles in the corner and everything else.' Despite whiskey rather than water in his corner, Jenkins stunned both the champion and the sporting world to take the crown from Ambers by a three-round TKO, 10 May 1940.

'I drank all the time when I was a kid,' Jenkins confessed. 'Never go to bed.' At $15,000–$25,000 a fight at that time with bourbon at $3.00 a bottle, the new champion could afford to indulge this and other of his habits. 'Cadillacs, I had about nine of them in 1940,' he recalled, 'four motorcycles, an airplane, and two racehorses ... Staying up all night, all them women ... I just beat myself up. The fighters didn't beat me. I did it myself.' This hardly assisted him in his first defence against future lightweight champion Bob Montgomery. 'I remember he really flattened me in the third round,' said Lew. 'As a matter of fact, the people got up to go home. I got up with them. I was laying flat on my face and the referee said, 'Eight'. I jumped up, cleared up real quick. I was young, full of energy. I made a monkey out of him. I won a decision.' Jenkins then took six rounds to flatten a man who'd previously done that to him, Peter Lello. But his notorious neglect of training made him an easy mark for the fists of Henry Armstrong, who KO'd him in six in a non-title contest. 1940 closed with a contest against Armstrong's conqueror, the new world welterweight champion, Fritzie Zivic, again non-title. Said Zivic:

> Jenkins was one of the gamest guys in the world. He couldn't fight too much, but what a dynamite puncher! … When he made a fist, never seen to this day knuckles, they stuck out this big. And when he put his gloves on, I found out later, he'd push the pads back so when you got hit with his punch all he had was a little bit of leather in between there … He hit me in the forehead in the first fight, I thought the building fell on me. If he'd hit me on the chin he'd have knocked me cold. Some think he won the fight, some think I won the fight. They called it a draw.

The battle-weary ex-champion, Lou Ambers, fatigued by the strain of making the weight, was sent into retirement by Jenkins in seven rounds, 28 February 1941, Madison Square Garden, New York. Lean and hungry future champion Bob Montgomery could not be accommodated so easily in a return match and an untrained, drunken Jenkins received a right pasting and lost the decision in this non-title contest. 'But I made it tough for myself,' Jenkins admitted, and subsequently proved the point further by crashing his motorcycle and breaking three vertebrae in his neck. This hardly helped him in his non-title contest against newly crowned welterweight champion Freddie 'Red' Cochrane. 'I had a cast on,' Jenkins said. 'Took it off before, then put it back on.' Cochrane won the decision.

On 19 December 1941, Lew put his crown on the line against leading contender Sammy Angott. He recalled:

> I was completely a cripple … it was just such a miserable

fight. I was painful all through it ... My grandma could beat him, honest to God. He couldn't even spell 'fight' as far as I was concerned. He would have went about two rounds with me ordinarily till I see that chance to throw that right hand. But I couldn't do that. I just didn't have it. Every time I'd try it almost blacked me out ... I never did anything right ... He beat me. He didn't beat me, but he won the fight. He was fighting a skeleton, bone, that's all I was.

The ex-champ had a dreadful year in 1942 when he lost nine out of ten fights. It was no disgrace to lose on points to future welterweight champion Marty Servo, but he should never have lost to never-wases such as Cosby Linson, Carmen Notch and John Thomas, the last by KO. Henry Armstrong repeated his knockout win and then there was a return with Fritzie Zivic. Jenkins's prospects weren't helped by the fact that a few days before the contest he'd got drunk and misbehaved and had then been blackjacked into insensibility by police officers. '... I stopped him, I think, in the ninth round,' said Zivic. 'I didn't knock him dead. I busted him up. They wanted to stop it in the sixth round because he was bleeding pretty good ... I said, "I don't care if you stop it. I like to see blood – somebody else's." Jenkins wanted to fight me in the dressing room. What a game guy he was ... I used to always tell people that he was the only fighter I know that could start a fight in an empty room.'

Jenkins hung up his gloves and joined the war effort, enlisting in the Coast Guard and being among the crew of the first landing craft to invade Normandy on D-Day in June 1944. On receiving an honourable discharge, he returned to the ring, beating ham 'n' eggers in 1946, remaining inactive in 1947, boxing once in 1948, winning thirteen and losing six in 1949. Then, on 6 March 1950, he fought future world welterweight and middleweight champion Carmen Basilio, Syracuse, New York. Many experts put Basilio in the lower half of the all-time welterweight Top Ten; but even though he lost the decision, Jenkins did not agree: 'That fricking bum, in my time I could knock him out in one round easy, and he's a big, strong guy ... I'm a little ol' worn-out man when I fought him. Washed up completely ... That was the end ... I said, *This fricking bum* ... Basilio was nothing of a fighter. He wasn't even in my class.'

After a knockout loss to former lightweight champion Beau Jack in April 1950, Jenkins returned to the army. There wasn't much else for him to do. He had lost both his wife and his money and though he was remarried with an infant son, his bouts of drunkenness didn't make him much of a husband and father. He was posted to the Korean War, 1951. There he found himself cut off behind enemy lines and surrounded by dead American bodies. Nevertheless, he made his way back to base where he was credited with having saved the lives of many fellow soldiers and subsequently decorated for gallantry. 'And, brother, I straightened out,' Jenkins stated. 'I lived a different life since then. That changed me. My wife and boy I wanted to get back to ... I finally got back to my line, brother, and seeing I was alive and realizing that I was alive, I said, "Oh, my God, I'm here, I'm back." And I wrote her right away on a piece of toilet paper.' Small wonder that New York reporter Charles Burton declared Lew to be 'America's original go, go, go man'.

Subsequently, Jenkins continued with a military career, retiring in 1963 as a first sergeant. Second World War and Korean veterans were treated rather better than the American victims of Vietnam and so he retired to modest comfort in Concord, California, near San Francisco, but supplemented his income and kept busy by driving a laundry truck. Looking back on his life, he was aware of his mistakes but his words about them should perhaps be etched upon his tombstone: 'I don't regret it.'

His successor, Sammy Angott, could hardly have been a greater contrast. Jenkins, whatever his vices, was an all-out, slam-bam action fighter. Angott was arguably the dullest boxer who ever lived. Nat Fleischer called him 'the first unpopular king of the class'. Fans hated the fact that he was not only excruciatingly tedious to watch, but he was also quite an effective ring technician. He could go round after round, making moves that were sound but utterly uninspiring, until his opponent blundered through boredom. It was virtually impossible to tag this clever ringman solidly and he clinched after virtually every blow he delivered. Lew Jenkins had become so exasperated by Angott's clutching tactics that he'd tried to toss him over his head.

The reign of the new champion, born 17 January 1915 in Washington, Pennsylvania, was not especially inspiring. One detects a certain disdain in Nat Fleischer's commentary: 'In his only defence of the crown against Allie Stolz in Madison Square Garden on May 15, 1942, he won a disputed split decision after being floored. Referee Frank Fullum, who voted for Stolz, took two rounds away from the challenger for low hitting and that saved Angott's crown. He retired soon afterwards.'

This threw the lightweight division into a state of confusion, exacerbated by the fact that the New York Commission and the National Boxing Association did not agree on anything. Both held separate tournaments to decide the championship issue. Beau Jack won the New York version by knocking out Tippy Larkin in 1.19 of the third round, 18 December 1942. Meanwhile, Luther 'Slugger' White defeated Willie Joyce on a unanimous decision at the Baltimore Coliseum, 4 January 1943, to win the recognition of the Maryland Commission. Sammy 'The Clutch' Angott announced his return to the ring and the NBA decided to recognize his bout with Slugger White as being for the world lightweight championship. Angott won this version of the title after fifteen unexciting rounds, 27 October 1943.

On 19 March 1943, Angott had engaged in a non-title contest with one of the greatest men ever to don a glove, world featherweight champion Willie Pep. Pep was such a brilliant, beautiful boxer that on one occasion he didn't throw a single punch during a round and just made a monkey out of his opponent, who couldn't lay a glove on him: *aficionados* sighed with pleasure at his superlative skill and the referee and judges gave that wondrous, non-violent round to Willie Pep. At the time he met Angott, Pep had run up an unprecedented streak of sixty-two consecutive victories. Angott proceeded to use his superior weight to smother all his style. He leaned on him and continuously tied him up in clinches, tiring him out to hand Pep his first loss via an unpopular ten-round decision. Pep went on to another winning streak of seventy-two victories with one draw, holding the featherweight title 1942–8 and 1949–50. Angott, tedious victor over this will-o'-the-wisp wizard, lost his NBA crown to Juan Zurita at Legion Stadium, Hollywood, California on 8 March 1944. Although this clever man was only knocked out once in 125 contests, few fans were sorry to see him go.

There is very little to be said about Juan Zurita. A tough Mexican southpaw born in Guadalajara, he won the NBA crown by decison over Sammy Angott, and he lost it on 18 April 1945, after five successive knockout victories, when he was himself kaoed in two rounds by the legendary Ike Williams.

The fight crowd paid more attention to the New York Commission than to the NBA. In those days, New York City *was* Boxing and legends were established at its shrine, Madison Square Garden. One such was Beau Jack, born Sidney Walker in Augusta, Georgia, 1 April 1927, who became a black shoeshine boy and earned extra nickels and dimes in the horrible spectacle known as the Battle Royal. White spectators still paid to see black youths punch out one another. The last one standing was the winner. 'We'd be blindfolded, and when the bell rang, you were on your own,' Beau Jack recalled. 'I won most of those things ... What I would do is swing from a deep crouch, way down where none of those wild swings could find me ... One night I made $25.'

His big break for better things began when he shined the two-toned, wing-tip shoes of gambler Bobby Jones, who had seen some of his amateur contests. Jones persuaded his golfing cronies to ante up $50 each for fifty shares in order to launch Beau Jack as a professional. The men who host the US Masters Golf Tournament were not disappointed in their investment. Within three years, Beau Jack had become a top contender and one of the hottest attractions in New York City. After defeating sterling contenders Terry Young and Allie Stolz, he KO'd Tippy Larkin to win New York recognition as lightweight champion.

Beau Jack always came to fight, taking his opponents' best shots with a joyous abandon, then coming back with his own non-stop combinations. He was easy to hit but that didn't seem to trouble him. He ignored advice to build a proper defence, relying instead on non-stop attack. He fought more times than any other boxer at the old Madison Square Garden on 49th Street and Eighth Avenue, a total of twenty-one contests, with gate receipts of $1,578,069, which should have gone into his bank account, but since horse-players Chick Wergeles and Bowman Milligan were his managers of record, it did not. He won thirteen contests and lost none in 1942, with eight inside the distance.

One of his victims was tough Fritzie Zivic, former welterweight champion, whom he decisioned twice in February and March, 1943. 'This is the man that I really learned a whole lot by fighting,' said Beau Jack. 'If you get in a clinch with this man and didn't do nothing you was ruined when you came out and this is what I learned.' That points win must have stood Beau Jack in good stead when he faced his boyhood hero, Henry Armstrong, and won that decision too. In later years, he always averred that the busiest fists were those of Henry Armstrong whilst Fritzie Zivic was 'the toughest and the roughest and knew what he was doing'.

On 21 May 1943 Beau Jack defended his crown against Bob

Montgomery, who was a slick counter-puncher and edged out the decision to take the title over a fifteen-round unanimous verdict. Six months later, on 19 November 1943, Beau Jack regained the New York version of the championship with a unanimous fifteen-round decision over Montgomery. Both bouts were packed with live action. Contenders Lulu Constantino and Maxie Berger were soundly defeated in January and February 1944, after which Beau Jack faced the NBA lightweight champion, Sammy Angott. This should have been for the right to hold the undisputed succession to the lightweight championship but unfortunately it was a non-title match. Although Beau Jack was his usual swinging but open self in trying to please the crowd and make a fight of it, Sammy Angott, whom Bert Sugar has called 'a tough, savvy boxer', was his usual dull but effective self and the contest was ruled a draw. The third match with Montgomery took place on 3 March 1944 and Beau Jack lost this one and his title via fifteen-round decision.

Beau Jack loved to fight and so he carried on. He beat lethal Al 'Bummy' Davis, whom he later called one of his hardest-hitting opponents. This was followed by a victory over NBA lightweight champion Juan Zurita. Clearly there was better fighting in New York. A rematch with old antagonist Bob Montgomery on 4 August 1944 saw Jack gain the ten-round decision but it was a non-title fight. Both men had by this time done a stint in the US Army and they fought on a War Bond drive. 'That was about the proudest thing that could happen to me in my life,' said Beau Jack.

After just one contest in 1945, he drew with and then decisioned contender Johnny Greco and in the same year, 1946, knocked out former NBA Champion, Sammy 'Clutch' Angott. Tragedy struck on 21 February 1947 when Jack faced smooth mover Tony Janiro. Beau Jack threw a left in the fourth round, missed badly and went down awkwardly to break his knee-cap, blaming it on a loose ring mat. The referee stopped the fight in Janiro's favour and Jack had to be carried to his corner. Even so, after an enforced nine-month layoff, he bounced back to KO future welterweight king Johnny Bratton in January 1948, and kept busy. A loss to Terry Young in February was followed by a win over Johnny Greco in April, and then revenge on points against Tony Janiro in May.

This qualified him for a match for the championship, 12 July 1948, against the great Ike Williams, who had by this time seized both the NBA and the New York versions of the championship. Williams iced Beau Jack in the sixth. 'Jack was a wide-open target,' Nat Fleischer observed mournfully. 'Ike Williams,' Beau Jack sighed, 'I couldn't get by this man. I don't know why. The better I got in shape, the worse I got beat. I just don't know how come I could never beat him. He was a great fighter, great champion, a good puncher, but not the hardest.' In three subsequent contests with Williams, Beau lost a decision, held the man to a draw and was knocked out.

By this time Beau Jack could still beat second-raters but he no longer had enough to cope with the top men. Future welterweight champion Kid Gavilan boxed circles around him in 1949. There was enough left for Beau Jack to KO fellow has-been Lew Jenkins in 1950 but he retired after being stopped by leading contender Gil Turner in 1951. The ill-advised comeback he made four years later saw him win two, draw one, and then be clobbered into retirement by his old nemesis, Ike Williams on an eighth-round KO.

'I loved boxing better than anything that I know but my family,' said Beau Jack; but the money had all gone and he returned to being a shoeshine boy, having his patch at the Fontainebleau Hotel, Miami Beach, Florida, for twenty years. He was a walking epitome of the old saying, 'From rags to riches to rags'. Yet he did not seem to be at all bitter. He gave interviews cheerful, fathered fifteen children in and out of his two marriages, trained boxers in the Miami gyms and walked back to his small apartment without the slightest complaint. According to one of his many sons, this is not a sordid tragedy at all. Beau Jack is still as fighting fit as a man of his years can be, he arouses respect every time he walks into the toughest of gyms and although he pretends to be poor, he has money salted away. Whilst other reports confirm the son's first two statements, the financial riddle is unlikely to be solved during his lifetime, and presently this happy warrior looks like blacking boots and living for quite a while yet.

Bob Montgomery, Jack's successor, was a less colourful figure but was nevertheless a worthy champion under the New York regime. Turning professional in 1938, this lithe, black man won his first twenty-four fights, with seventeen KO's. On 18 February 1944 at Madison Square Garden, New York, top contender Montgomery took a tune-up against vicious Al 'Bummy' Davis. The odds favoured Montgomery at 10–1. The bell rang. Davis threw a wild right, which missed by a mile. Montgomery grabbed Davis's arm and tried to spin him, only to be socked by Davis's left and floored. He arose groggily, walked into another Davis left and was counted out in just sixty-three seconds.

Fortunately for Bob Montgomery, this was not a title fight, but his 4 August 1947 defence in Philadelphia against the NBA champion, Ike Williams, was. A photograph in front of me shows Montgomery twisted on the ropes in visible agony as Williams belts him in the balls. This may or may not have been revenge for the body punching which had won Montgomery a twelve round KO victory over Williams back in 1944. On this occasion, Williams destroyed the New York claimant in six rounds, unified the title at last, brought order into a chaotic scene with some of the deadliest lightweight punching ever witnessed; and who later said, 'The lightweight title's the greatest thing I ever had.'

NOTE TO CHAPTER TEN

LEW JENKINS
Lightweight champion of the world: 1940–1.
Total bouts: 109.
Won: 65 (47 by KO; 18 by decision).
Lost: 39 (12 by KO; 27 by decision).
Draws: 5.

SAMMY ANGOTT
Lightweight champion of the world: 1941–2.
NBA lightweight champion of the world: 1943–4.
Total Bouts: 125.
Won: 94 (22 by KO; 72 by decision).
Lost: 23 (1 by KO; 22 by decision).
Draws: 8.

JUAN ZURITA
NBA lightweight champion of the world: 1945.
Total bouts: 138.
Won: 115 (38 by KO, 76 by decision, 1 by foul).
Lost: 21 (7 by KO; 14 by decision).
Draws: 2.

BEAU JACK
New York Commission lightweight champion of the
world: 1942–3; 1943–4.
Total Bouts: 111.
Won: 83 (40 by KO; 43 by decision).
Lost: 23 (3 by KO; 20 by decision).
Draws: 5.

BOB MONTGOMERY
NYC lightweight champion of the world: 1943; 1944–7.
Total bouts: 97.
Won: 75 (37 by KO; 38 by decision).
Lost: 19 (3 by KO; 16 by decision).
Draws: 3.

11

From Racing Demon to Old Bones

'Boy, Ike Williams could'a powdered him any time,' hard-bitten veterans were saying in tough fight gyms twenty years after the reign of Ike Williams ended, when watching young and hopeful contenders. Most experts regard him as having been the greatest lightweight champion of his generation. He moved so swiftly that it was hard to tag him with a serious punch, though when one landed, he could take it; meanwhile he had knockout power in either fist. One false move and Ike Williams could cold-cock the man in front of him.

This warrior, whose words could be as bitter as his blows, was born on 2 August 1923 in Georgia but moved to Trenton, New Jersey. He turned professional boxer at just sixteen years of age on 15 March 1940. Although he lost four contests to more experienced men in his first four years, he won forty-one fights, and in 1942–3 went twenty-nine straight victories without a loss. That streak was ended in Philadelphia on 25 January 1944 by the former and future NYC lightweight champion Bob Montgomery. 'He knocked me out that night. No excuses,' Williams admitted. 'Maybe he'd have beaten me anyway. One thing, I felt he fought me very dirty. He's the only fighter that ever fought me dirty ... he knocked me out with eleven seconds to go ... Montgomery, he used his head on me, that's the way he fought me dirty and I was a naïve kid then.'

Williams came roaring back to the ring. 'I lost several fights coming up,' he confessed unashamedly, 'but every time I lost a fight I learned something.' He won two victories over awkward ex-champ Sammy Angott. He swopped decisions with leading contender Willie Joyce. Wins over contenders of the calibre of Lulu Constantino, Cleo Shans, Maxie Berger and Dorsie Lay qualified him for a challenge against NBA lightweight champion Juan Zurita on 18 April 1945 in Mexico City.

In the second round, Williams hit Zurita with a perfect right to the body and a dazzling left to the jaw and the champion was stretched out stiff for the final count. A riot ensued. Bricks were thrown into the ring. When Williams tried to pick up his championship belt, a Mexican pulled a gun on him. 'I saw the belt maybe for five minutes,' Williams recalled sourly. 'I haven't seen it since. Maybe it's down in Mexico City now.' He discovered that in winning one version of the world championship his troubles were only just beginning. Mexican thugs followed him to the airport.

Worse was to come. Williams had tired of the exploitative and drunkenly incompetent ways of his manager, Connie McCarthy, and wanted to end their business arrangement. 'That's when he ran to the Boxing Guild,' Williams sighed. 'They started in 1946, to keep fighters "in line". Like, any fighter that tried to leave his manager, they were going to blackball him ... World champion and couldn't get a fight!' According to Williams, no manager or promoter dared deal with him for months because to do so would mean ostracism by the increasingly unsavoury powers that had moved in during the war to control boxing. Eventually, Williams had precious little alternative except to sign a contract with a gangster named Blinky Palermo. This gave Williams the fights he needed: the money went to Palermo.

The mental stress and strain affected the performance of Ike Williams. Non-title fights saw him drop a decision to Willie Joyce and although he beat Gene Burton, he suffered a KO loss to – of all people – boring Sammy Angott, whom he'd already defeated twice. One wonders just how much money the well-connected gamblers made on these fights. 'But I didn't know anything about the man's reputation,' Williams later protested regarding Blinky Palermo. That's rather like a Chicago Prohibition beer brewer declaring that he knew nothing about Al Capone.

However, Williams had a much better year in 1946, when he beat future welterweight champion Johnny Bratton, KO'd tough contender Enrique Bolanos and travelled to Cardiff, Wales, to lay his crown on the line against skilful British champion Ronnie James. Williams baffled observers by doing very little for the first eight rounds other than shuffling around the ring and slipping punches. Ronnie James was looking classy and way ahead on all scorecards when the bell rang for the ninth. James came out to jab nimbly. He never saw the punch which started from Williams's right shoulder, seemed to twitch backward as though it were a feint, then whipped downward in a perfect arc to strike deep into James's liver. James dropped as though he'd been shot. Although he somehow managed to stagger to his feet, he was now easy meat for the champion, who finished him fast. The British boxing crowd was aghast at seeing this lethal but legal punch, unknown hitherto in British boxing rings: it was the 'bolo', well developed from the Joe Gans and Battling Nelson days by middleweight Ceferino Garcia, but executed to perfection by Ike Williams.

It is hard to understand how Williams could have dropped a non-title decision to former victim Gene Burton, but that happened in 1947, the year he also stopped Tippy Larkin and fulfilled his dream of a rematch with his former conqueror, Bob Montgomery, NYC lightweight champion, for the undisputed crown. Williams later claimed that he had only signed with Blinky Palermo because the man had promised him a return go with Montgomery. Philadelphia on 4 August 1947 was the venue for this savage contest. Montgomery hurt Williams in the early rounds with a vicious body attack, fighting out of a crouch. Williams waited patiently for him to straighten out of that crouch for just one instant, then caught him immaculately and knocked him flat on his back. Although Montgomery made it to his unsteady feet, it was all Williams after that. Montgomery was finished by a mean combination to both head and body in the sixth round. One of those blows at least definitely landed low. 'I got revenge with Montgomery,' said Williams. 'As far as I'm concerned, the thing's forgotten. But I guess he still holds a little animosity against me.'

Ike Williams was now universally recognized as undisputed lightweight champion of the world and he had undeniably paid his dues on the way there. 'That was the biggest night of my life when I won that fight,' he stated. In 1948, he seemed invincible. Kid Gavilan, the great future welterweight champion and a fellow-master of the bolo punch, lost the decision to Williams on 27 February. There was a fifteen-round points victory over Enrique Bolanos on 25 May. Beau Jack was slaughtered in six rounds, 12 July, and Jesse Flores was iced in September.

These were splendidly convincing performances but Williams was starting to have problems in making the lightweight limit. Although he earned around $250,000 in 1948, 'I did a first-class job of managing my money real bad.'

As far as one can discern, he never asked Blinky Palermo about all the deductions for 'expenses' and was even foolish enough to lend him $10,000. 'So then I went to him about my money, he started crying about he's broke, and he's going to get his brains blown out if he didn't pay some people, he said he needed my purses to pay off some old debts.' One wishes that Blinky Palermo could have been put in the ring with Ike Williams, but corruption, not courage, was Blinky's line in trade. Meanwhile the champion was doing himself no favours by dropping huge bets on the golf course. He was also being far too generous with his handouts to an entourage of parasites.

If he was slipping slightly, this was only occasionally apparent, and then only in non-title contests. Future welterweight champion Johnny Bratton was again decisioned in 1949, though this was followed by a close loss on points to the great Kid Gavilan. A title defence on 21 June 1949 saw Williams execute a perfect KO over old foe Enrique Bolanos in the fourth round. 'I fought the greatest fight I ever fought in my life,' Williams asserted. 'I felt like I could have fought forever ... It was a right hand to the body. He went down slowly. He was as knocked out as any fighter ever was. That's the fight that I would have bet my life on that I would have whipped any lightweight who ever lived that night...'

In 1950, Williams once again knocked out future welterweight champion Johnny Bratton – he always had this man's number – defeated John L Davis and swopped decisions with Joe Miceli. The following year saw him win three bouts by KO, drop a decision to Miceli, then win over Beau Jack and Fritzie Pruden. After a six-year reign as world lightweight champion, he defended his title against Jimmy Carter in Madison Square Garden, 25 May 1951. This sixth defence was plagued by Williams's problems in making the weight and by torn muscles in a freak sparring accident which temporarily crippled Ike's ability to throw an effective right. 'I was so tired from losing weight that the last two or three rounds I couldn't even throw a punch,' said Williams. Carter knocked Williams down twice and in the tenth round, sent him flying through the ropes. Referee Pete Scalzo rightly stopped the slaughter in the fourteenth. 'It's just as well,' Williams commented, 'because I might have gotten hurt.' He added: 'I been going down ever since that.'

The ex-champ boxed on in a 'win some, lose some' kind of way. Leading contender Gil Turner stopped him in ten. Although he won two contests in 1952, he was KO'd by the white 'made for TV' contender, Chuck Davey. In January 1953 he faced Carmen Basilio, who would win the welterweight championship twice and then defeat Sugar Ray Robinson for the middleweight crown.

Said Basilio:

It was a tough fight. This guy was supposed to be on his way down but he was a hard puncher. I got a vicious cut in that fight. It took about six stitches to close the cut ... The referee ... I think it was Petey Scalzo – he gave me 10 out of 10. But I had to be on my toes even though I won 10 out of 10 ... They say Robinson was the hardest puncher pound for pound. I've got to go with Ike Williams. Pound for pound, this guy had to be the hardest puncher. He was a vicious puncher even then when I fought him.

Basilio won a unanimous ten-round decision.

After a draw with and a KO over Beau Jack, whose style he knew and had always mastered, Ike Williams retired from the ring. His subsequent career is a sad and familiar story. His management had taken most of his money. He made bad investments. He had to return to regular employment. After a stint with the New Jersey Conservation Department, he became an aeroplane maintenance supervisor at McGuire Air Force Base, and then a labourer at a New Jersey job training centre. He couldn't even afford to go to the fights at Madison

Square Garden where he had once been the star attraction, although its promotional head, Teddy Brenner, was usually kind enough to give him a ticket. His reputation was still hot in the fight gyms but it faded in the memory of the fight crowds as the years went by. Peter Dooley recalled an occasion in the 1970s at the Garden:

> When it was time for the main go, Johnny Addie introduced a few current fighters who were in attendance. Then 'Ladies and Gentlemen, the former lightweight champion of the world … Ike Williams.' The man in the worn-out suit came up from the audience, climbed through the ropes, waved his hand and went to each of the boxers' corners. There wasn't much applause, much less a thundering ovation. Ike Williams got a polite, warm reception from the Madison Square Garden crowd. A tribute to a memory.

Williams's conqueror would have been lucky to receive even utterly polite applause. Jimmy Carter was a tough and skilful professional whose punches were planted cruelly, yet he kindled no legend. Aficionados could not deny him respect but tended to regard him as being rather like a master plumber doing a good job. This New York city resident had been born on 15 December 1923 in Aiken, South Carolina. On 1 April 1952, he decisioned the rugged Mexican Lauro Salas, then met him again on 14 May, at Los Angeles' Olympic Auditorium. This time Salas took a split decision and the title.

Salas, born in Mexico in 1927, and then boxing out of Monterey, had been a professional fighter since the age of fourteen. He won renown for his extraordinary durability and his jolting left hook throughout his career but his technical errors left him open to heavy punishment. Nevertheless, he was Mexico's first world champion; and the hungry boy who'd fought for a few pesos was now hugged publicly by

President Aleman as both men wept. 'I champion of all Mexico!' Salas exulted. 'The world, you fool, the world!' yelled his American manager. This idyll lasted for just six months and two weeks before Jimmy Carter took back the title on October 15 1952 via unanimous decision at Chicago Stadium.

Paddy DeMarco beat Carter by fifteen-round decision to ascend the throne on 5 March 1954 at Madison Square Garden. This man, born 10 February 1928 in Brooklyn, was a strong but uninspiring brawler. He received quite a beating in the return match at the Cow Palace, San Francisco, 17 November 1954, and was stopped at 0.14 of the fifteenth round. Carter, the unprecedented but unlauded three-time champion, then lost the crown to underdog Wallace Bud Smith via fifteen-round decision, Boston, 29 June 1955. Smith defended his title successfully against Carter in Cincinnati on 19 October but lost it at the Municipal Stadium, New Orleans, 24 August 1956, to veteran Joe 'Old Bones' Brown.

This period of the worthy and competent Carter, Salas, DeMarco, Smith and Brown has to be called one of the most uninspiring in lightweight boxing history. Sandy Saddler, one of the greatest featherweight champions 1948–9 and 1950–7, knocked out Joe Brown and drew with Jimmy Carter in 1947. He stopped Paddy DeMarco in nine rounds, 1949, though he did drop two decisions to him in 1951. Strong Lauro Salas was a Saddler KO victim twice, in 1950 and 1951. It doesn't say much for the lightweight kings that they had fallen victim to a featherweight, albeit one of the greatest of all time. One sports writer lamented: 'lightweights, my lightweights, where have you gone?'

It didn't help the sport that organized crime was tightening its grip. Ike Williams was hardly the only warrior who was robbed. The Mafia contracted a profitable alliance with James D Norris, a multi-millionaire who had inherited his father's grain fortune. Norris, who had already invested in horse-racing, ice shows and hockey, now approached Mike Jacobs, New York's promotional czar, but now ageing and ailing, and bought out his interests to form the International Boxing Club (IBC). With his gangster friends, Frankie Carbo and Blinky Palermo, Norris now had a choke hold on Madison Square Garden, the princpal arenas in Chicago, St Louis, Indianapolis, Washington, Omaha, Massachusetts – and on a vital new factor in this profitable equation: television.

Mike Jacobs had foreseen this development when he had told fighter Fritzie Zivic: 'you'll see the day when two thousand people will see a fight in a stadium and twenty million will watch it on television in their homes.' 'I thought he was nuts,' Zivic reminisced, 'but he was right. Boy, was he right!' Unfortunately, Jacobs – who, whatever his faults, wanted the contests to be on the level – was too old and ill to take advantage of his remarkable perception. Norris and friends were not.

Media matters had been pioneered by King C Gillette, originally an unsuccessful door-to-door salesman of his patented 'safety razor'. His breakthrough had come in 1901 when he gave away a free holder to anyone who bought the blades and popularized the notion of self-shaving at home rather than going to the barber. He used baseball stars to endorse his advertising and triumphed by selling his invention to 4,500,000 American servicemen as standard issue in the First World War. This gave Gillette the money to essay gambles, sponsoring a radio show on sports in 1929, then backing the Jim Braddock–Max Baer heavyweight championship contest in 1935. By 1940, 'The Gillette Cavalcade of Sports' had purchased rights to the Kentucky Derby, the NFL championship, the Orange Bowl and the East-West football game. On 26 September 1944, Mike Jacobs sold Gillette the rights to televise the Willie Pep–Chalky Wright world featherweight championship plus the next fifty boxing cards at Madison Square Garden and St Nicholas Arena.

Gillette's *Friday Night Fights* would be on the air for the next nineteen years.

True, there were hiccups along the way, especially when advertising rights were sub-contracted. Pabst Beer, for instance, once demanded that lightweight champion Wallace Bud Smith be taken off the bill because he was thought to be advertising Budweiser beer. A CBS executive decided to take the advice of the Pabst beer commercials on another occasion, which was to have a beer after every round: the fight ended by KO in the tenth but the executive had been flattened by the ninth. An advertising executive listened impassively to a superb analysis of the second Willie Pep–Sandy Saddler fight by a leading boxing expert, explaining in detail precisely why Saddler lost that fight. 'You can't say that sort of thing on the air,' the ad man grunted, 'because the minute you say that Saddler is doing something wrong, you're using a negative approach, and you can't do that. You're knocking the show.'

The march of TV into people's homes was inexorable and there seemed to be an endless appetite for boxing in America during the 1950s, mostly on prime time. Monday: St Nicholas and Eastern Parkway arenas courtesy of DuMont; Tuesday: Sunnyside Gardens, New York; Wednesday: fights sponsored by Pabst Blue Ribbon beer from all over the nation; Thursday: the fights in Newark, New Jersey were carried coast to coast; Friday: Gillette took pride of place on NBC; and on Saturday, ABC employed legendary trainer Ray Arcel to comment on its fight shows.

Naturally, Jim Norris and his IBC consortium invested heavily in television. The medium had mixed effects upon the sport. On the good side, it furthered its popularity and brought it to many who would never have dreamed of going to a boxing match. It gave fighters the public exposure they needed and (strictly on paper) better pay days. Norris also pioneered the new phenomenon of closed-circuit TV in cinemas. All this would eventually result in multi-million dollar bonanzas, seen by tens of millions all over the globe.

It had its dark side too, though. The old, small fight clubs which had nourished the sport and given education to its aspiring young hopefuls, were driven out of business. Few wanted to pay for a minor local contest when they could see a televised major bout for free. The IBC held a virtual monopoly over the sport in America and promoters, managers and boxers who did not comply with its edicts were blacklisted and could barely scratch a living. Frankie 'Mr Gray' Carbo and Blinky Palermo could get away with murder and did. 'There's always been larceny in boxing,' the insufferably cantankerous but wholly honest Dan Parker wrote in the New York *Mirror*, 'and when I've seen it, I've written it. But it's worse now than ever before.' It is hardly surprising that cynics took to calling the IBC 'Octopus Incorporated'.

A further disturbing effect of TV was to lower the standard of understanding of the sport. The present writer is highly appreciative of the medium for arousing his initial enraptured enthusiasm as a boy and perpetuating it for him as a man, allowing him to view many contests he would never otherwise have been able to witness. In my view, the good far outweighs the bad; but the ills have to be recognized. In their endeavours to sell consumer goods and boxing to a public largely ignorant of the sport's finer points, the sponsors and advertising agencies manufactured fighters 'made for TV'. For example, there was white Chuck Davey, whose 'boy next door' looks far exceeded his fistic talents and who won some surprising victories over experienced black veterans. Paid commentators were also circumscribed in what they could actually say. This certainly isn't true of honest and acute Don Dunphy, who commented on the Gillette fights in the manner of a true expert, but other commentators were less scrupulous, spoke the lines scripted for them to build up a fighter and misled a naive audience.

There was so much money at stake with the entry of TV, and live gates were falling. 1946 had seen thirty-three dates at

Madison Square Garden draw 406,681 fans to pay $2,062,000: 1952 witnessed twenty Garden bouts attracting just 137,381 punters paying $435,450, a loss of over $1,600,000. Moreover, during those years, nine of of ten small fight clubs went out of business. The IBC lost more than $1,500,000 on live gates on eighty cards in one year but the directors cried all the way to the bank as they more than made up for it in TV revenue. Connected gamblers made fortunes too. Mr Joe Q Public shaved himself with a Gillette razor blade, then sat down with a Pabst Blue Ribbon beer to enjoy the spectacle of the fights in his living room. There was benefit for everybody except the boxers.

Some clean, fresh air blew into this stinking scene with the Senate Committee Hearings on Organized Crime in Interstate Commerce, chaired by Senator Estes Kefauver, which found that Jim Norris had flagrantly associated – surprise! surprise! – with known gangsters such as Frankie Carbo and Blinky Palermo. These mobsters were charged – surprise! surprise! – with fixing fights, some of which involved renowned boxers. The US Justice Department's Anti-Trust division took up the case and in 1957, a court ruling found Norris and his IBC guilty of monopolistic practices, forcing him to sell his $2,500,000 share in Madison Square Garden, unload other stock in New York and Chicago, dissolve the IBC and retire from his involvement in boxing. Only the corrupt mourned the fact.

Some dignity was restored to the lightweight championship by the unlikely, gaunt figure of Joe 'Old Bones' Brown, who had taken a tarnished crown in August 1956. Although Sandy Saddler, who had beaten him in 1947, later called him 'a very good fighter', Brown had endured an erratic ring career, causing him to retire on a number of occasions. Born poor in Baton Rouge, Louisiana, 18 May 1926, Brown had been exploited and never really got a break until he met Wallace Bud Smith for the title. There was bad luck once again for Brown that night, for he broke his right hand in the third, yet his exceptionally fast left jab enabled him to win the decision and the title.

Once he was champion, confidence returned to a man formerly so disheartened that he'd lost a number of contests he should easily have won. At the age of thirty, he finally came into his own, showing himself to be among the finest lightweight champions of all time. He could go the distance, he could take a punch, though usually his skills ensured that he didn't have to, and he could punch. His left jab was swift if not powerful, but good timing gave him a jolting left hook and his right could flatten any man at his weight. He was a clever ring strategist who boxed with guile, then suddenly exploded with sizzling savagery. He would reign for six years and defend his title eleven times – a record no champion at his weight had surpassed.

He started by giving Wallace Bud Smith a return bout at Miami Beach, 13 February 1957, and disposed of him easily in the eleventh. Orlando Zulueta of Cuba was the next contender, 'the fighter with knives in his gloves'. Nobody could figure out how Zulueta managed to cut virtually every man he ever fought but Brown knocked him out at Denver, Colorado, in the fifteenth round on 19 June. The following year saw the champion engage in three non-title contests and two title defences. The non-title affairs had him icing Cuba's champion, Orlando Echevarria, in less than a round as part of the inaugural programme of the spanking new Sports Stadium in Havana; flattening Ernie Williams in five; and dropping an upset ten-round decision to Johnny Busso in the newly built auditorium at Miami Beach. When the crown was at stake, he smashed skilful Ralph Dupas to the canvas with an immaculate right swish in the eighth round, Houston, 7 May 1958, then prepared to face the formidable Kenny Lane.

Madison Square Garden matchmaker Teddy Brenner called Kenny Lane of Michigan 'the greatest southpaw lightweight who ever lived'. A fierce challenge was mounted in Houston on 23 July. Lane was a tough slugger, reminiscent of Battling

Nelson, and he never stopped crowding Brown and preventing him from getting set. Brown's wickedly accurate punches crushed Lane's nose, but with blood all over his body, Lane stormed back with body punching, sending an open-mouthed Brown back to his corner and gasping for air.

Most boxers dislike fighting a left-hander. This is because he does everything the other way around, coming in with his right arm extended and cocking a deadly left. The southpaw is used to fighting men with the customary stance. The right-hander is perplexed by the moves of the unusual. By the tenth round, Brown was trailing but he rallied to pile up the points. Many had it even going into the fifteenth and final round. 'Take it easy, coast,' Doc Kearns, former manager of Jack Dempsey advised Kenny Lane, adding: 'You got him. Don't get knocked out.' Brown gave his all and was rewarded by a unanimous decision. The national TV audience disputed the verdict. This may have been because they or the commentator could not discern Brown's neater, niftier work in the later rounds or else they were biased by the fact that Lane was white and Brown was black. In any event, it was a close call and afterwards Brown shook his head and sighed wearily, 'No more southpaws.'

Recovering speedily from this ordeal, Brown boxed a non-title draw with top contender Joey Lopes so as to feel him out, then tore him to bits when they met for the title in Chicago, 4 December, 1957, flooring him in the seventh and polishing him off in the eleventh. 'Old Bones' was named 'Fighter of the Year' in 1958, avenging the previous year's loss to Johnny Busso with his title on the line, then stopping Paolo Rosi in eight. He closed the year with six wins, no losses and one draw with Joey Parks, which he'd avenged in their return bout. A more demanding challenge was that of Dave Charnley, one of the best lightweights that England has ever produced. Brown's old bones must have groaned when told that he was a southpaw.

'He was a wicked body puncher,' Henry Cooper said of

Dave Charnley, with whom he had trained, 'a very cold little fighter, spiteful with it. His eyes were like steel. He was so determined.' He had wrecked British welterweight champion Peter Waterman so badly that the latter never fought again. He had emulated Brown in destroying Joey Lopes. Now Charnley travelled to Houston, determined to wrest the crown from Joe Brown. Harry Carpenter forecast a Charnley victory, calling the Englishman 'a midget Marciano who had only once failed to spank a Yank'. 'I'm doing this guy Charnley a favour,' Joe Brown responded, 'I hate them lefties. I'd get more money fighting other guys.' The challenger was mean in training, refusing to see his wife except at meal times. The champion was equally mean as he trained in a pine camp. 'A man gets lonely and fit out here to kill,' he told Reg Gutteridge.

When the bell rang for the first round, Brown danced out to spear Charnley with his snake-like left. His gaunt body with its dancer's hips and his spindly arms were quite a contrast to Charnley's muscular, stocky build. Observers should have noticed the bulging biceps of Brown and the lean, fit muscle on his long legs. He used his superior reach to keep Charnley at long range, frustrating his endeavours at in-fighting, Charnley's strength. By the fifth, Brown was easily ahead and had blacked Charnley's eye. Charnley swarmed in recklessly, staggered Brown with a right and forced him into a fierce exchange, to his subsequent cost. Brown hit him with an uppercut and, as he ducked to avoid the counter, there was a clash of heads which gashed Charnley's right eyebrow beyond redemption. He had to quit in his corner. English reporters waxed lyrical over England's gallant loss. Not so America's Jimmy Cannon who wrote: 'Brown acted with the boredom of a tavern keeper rousting a stormy drunk.'

It was a different story on 18 April 1961, when a $50,000 purse lured Joe Brown to London for a rematch with Charnley at the Earl's Court arena. This contest recalled the glorious days of Gans and Battling Nelson. Basic strategy was established from the start. Brown went head-hunting and Charnley tried to tear apart that tall, lean body. Brown blocked the blows with his elbows but Charnley's assault was so rapid and furious that at times the champion was left staggering. Brown's spear-like left just couldn't keep Charnley away from him, so suddenly, mid-way through the fifth, he fired a right that landed on Charnley's nose with an audible *crack*. Blood cascaded from the bridge of Charnley's nose but he fought back with ferocious vim and vigour, forcing Brown to back up against the ropes and play his game in trading punches. Now the rounds alternated, Charnley winning some on incredible velocity of aggression and Brown, forced out of the customary craftsmanlike style that had won him the early rounds, coming back with dazzling two-fisted combinations that were almost but not quite enough to finish his determined challenger. Non-stop two-fisted short hooking won Charnley the thirteen and fourteenth rounds, then he went all out for a knockout in the fifteenth, leaning on Brown in a clinch on the ropes as the final bell rang. Respected British referee Tommy Little gave the decision to champion Joe Brown, presumably on account of his early, solid lead – but there was something close to a riot among the spectators. Harry Carpenter said publicly on BBC TV that he thought that Charnley had been robbed.

Winner and still champion Joe Brown returned enriched to America and another challenger, Puerto Rico's Carlos Ortiz, on 21 April 1962, Las Vegas, Nevada. According to Ortiz:

He was a murderous puncher. I was scared stiff. Not actually scared, but nervous as you can be ... I knew that Brown was a good puncher, that he was a good left hooker, terrific body puncher, good boxer, but I was going to outfox him. He thought that I was going to go in, because of his age ... he thought that I was going to go in and try to take him out fast because he was old and because I was younger ... But I changed my tactics.

From the first round on I said, *I'm just going to box this guy, let him come to me. I'm gonna change tactics ...* But for fourteen rounds Joe Brown was trying to knock me out with a right hand and he could never do it because he was not ready for my type of fight.

Ortiz, pioneering the new style of the Sixties, won thirteen out of fifteen rounds against Brown, a professor of the Forties, and walked away with the crown.

'Old Bones' continued to punch for pay. On 25 February 1963, he faced his old foe Dave Charnley in Manchester, England. By this time, Brown was thirty-seven, ten years older than Charnley, but he had only ever lost one bout in 118 by KO. Dave Charnley, however, was merciless that night in exacting his revenge. He crowded him until the sixth, when Brown made a fatal error of concentration. Charnley saw the opening and smashed a short right to the jaw that left Brown dazedly blinking as his guard folded, then followed through with a devastating body hook. Brown sank bewilderedly for the count.

Although Brown did not hang up his gloves until 1970, his later contests were without distinction. In common with so many boxers of his era, he had been thieved of the money due to him, and such little as he had received, he had wasted. This illustrious luminary of the ring, whose record for title defences has not been beaten, sank into obscurity and his eventual fate is not known.

The evils and corruption attendant upon boxing would not by any means come to an end with the accession to the lightweight throne of Carlos Ortiz, but in the ring Joe Brown had inspired what would turn out to be a brief but noble era of elegance.

NOTE TO CHAPTER ELEVEN

IKE WILLIAMS
Lightweight champion of the world: 1945–51 (NBA); 1947–51 (undisputed).
Total bouts: 153.
Won: 124 (60 by KO; 64 by decision).
Lost: 24 (6 by KO; 18 by decision).
Draws: 5.

JIMMY CARTER
Lightweight champion of the world: 1951–2; 1952–4; 1954–5.
Total bouts: 120.
Won: 81 (31 by KO; 50 by decision).
Lost: 30 (3 by KO; 27 by decision).
Draws: 9.

LAURO SALAS
Lightweight champion of the world: 1952.
Total bouts: 148.
Won: 83 (39 by KO; 44 by decision).
Lost: 52 (7 by KO; 44 by decision, 1 by foul).
Draws: 12.
No Decision: 1.

PADDY DE MARCO
Lightweight champion of the world: 1954.
Total bouts: 104.
Won: 75 (8 by KO; 67 by decision).
Lost: 26 (7 by KO; 19 by decision).
Draws: 3.

WALLACE BUD SMITH

Lightweight champion of the world: 1955–6.
Total bouts: 60.
Won: 31 (18 by KO; 13 by decision).
Lost: 23 (7 by KO; 16 by decision).
Draws: 6.

JOE BROWN

Lightweight champion of the world: 1956–62.
Total bouts: 160.
Won: 104 (48 by KO; 56 by decision).
Lost: 42 (9 by KO; 32 by decision; 1 by foul).
Draws: 12.
No Contest: 2.

12

An Era of Elegance

Something very strange happened in a Miami gym in 1960. Ingemar Johansson, heavyweight champion of the world, needed a sparring partner and a young man called Cassius Clay volunteered for the job. Clay had won a gold medal as a light-heavyweight, Rome Olympic Games, that year and had only recently turned professional, so no observer regarded him as anything other than a skinny kid who could sharpen up the champion's moves. Clay amazed them by making Johansson look so clumsy and foolish that the session had to be stopped after the second round. Johansson went on to lose his title back to Floyd Patterson. Clay went on to become the great Muhammad Ali. There is a sting in this tale.

The best boxers of previous generations were teaching all the wisdom of their craft in the best gyms. They often deplored the youngsters' lack of dedication to training. What surprised them, however, was that some of these youngsters

126

were coming up with innovations of their own which had never been seen before. One can compare these veterans to Picasso's art teacher, who was delighted by the perfect classical portrait of a woman that his pupil painted at the age of seventeen, only to be horrified by Picasso's subsequently sensational experimentation. For Cassius Clay, as he then was, cannot be called the only improviser of new techniques. Carlos Ortiz of Puerto Rico was honing new skills too.

There are accepted moves in boxing and each move has its counter. Victory often goes to the man who discerns a split-second error of concentration or physical co-ordination. However, a boxer becomes confused if he is confronted with moves that he has never encountered in the gym. Ortiz bewildered his opponents in racking up twenty-seven straight victories.

He was born to Puerto Rico, 9 September 1936, then emigrated to New York with his family in quest of a better life and turned professional at eighteen. His first loss was via decision to leading contender Johnny Busso on 27 June 1958 but he avenged it three months later. On 28 October 1958, he travelled to London to fight Great Britain's outstanding Dave Charnley, 'the midget Marciano' who would give champion Joe Brown so much pain. The steely Charnley just couldn't cope with the innovations of Ortiz and was outboxed easily over ten rounds. Kenny Lane, however, had an answer to the techniques of Ortiz on 31 December. He simply walked in, took every shot that Ortiz had to throw and never stopped punching to win the decision. Ortiz came back with a sensational KO over ferocious Len Matthews in his home town of Philadelphia and shouted for a title shot against reigning champion Joe Brown.

He shouted in vain but the Madison Square Garden matchmaker, Teddy Brenner, came up with a good idea. Why not revive the junior welterweight championship, which had fallen into disuse since the Thirties? This division still exists today and the World Boxing Council calls it super lightweight. 'I said I never heard of that title before and I didn't think it had any importance,' Ortiz stated, but added: 'I said: "Sure, why not?" ' His opponent was his former conqueror, fierce Kenny Lane. Said Ortiz:

> In the first round I knocked Kenny down. I was real strong, you know. I almost took him out in the first round. In the second round I hit him the hardest right hand shot I ever hit a boxer before, right on the eye. I opened his eye up so bad that the doctor had to stop the fight and I became the junior welterweight champion ... I really wanted the lightweight title because it was a recognized title and that's what I wanted.

Although Ortiz wanted the lightweight championship there was still his own title to defend, which he did on February 4 1960 in Los Angeles by knocking out Battling Torres in the tenth. On 15 June in San Francisco, he won the decision against Italy's Duilio Loi, then journeyed to Milan to face him in a rematch. Boxers are cynical about visits to Italy and there is a saying in the gyms: 'If you knock him out, with luck you might get a draw.' Duilio Loi took his title by decision on 1 September 1960 and repeated a questionable points win in Milan, 10 May 1961.

Nevertheless, the dream of Ortiz was finally fulfilled when he took the lightweight championship away from the outstanding Joe Brown through superlative boxing skill, 21 April 1962, Las Vegas. 'I never thought that a person could feel so good, so glad, so happy,' said Ortiz, 'because I was trying for a long time, so when that moment finally came I cried and I was so happy.' Unfortunately, the recognition of Carlos Ortiz was nearly but not quite universal. For reasons best known to itself, the Michigan State Boxing Commission chose to recognize a bout between its favourite son, tough Kenny Lane, and one Paul Armstead at Veterans Memorial Park, Saginaw, as being for the title. When Lane won by fifteen-round unanimous decision, the Michigan authorities announced him to be the lightweight champion of the world, 18 August 1963.

Carlos Ortiz initially ignored this fatuous nonsense, though he was ready and willing to be a fighting champion. 'I think I was the only champion that helped boxing so much,' he declared in later years. 'You know why? Because I gave a chance to all the fighters, all the good contenders, and I went into their backyard ... I think I was the only champion who traveled worldwide defending my title.' This was not exactly true. For instance, there had been globe-trotters Freddie Miller at featherweight and Panama Al Brown at bantam-weight during the Thirties; and soon enough there would be Muhammad Ali at heavyweight. But it is undeniable that Carlos Ortiz was willing to travel in order to face all the finest contenders of his time.

Tokyo, December 1962: Ortiz knocked out Teruo Kosaka. In Puerto Rico, 7 April 1963, Ortiz stopped Doug Valliant. After two non-title victories, it was a date at Manila, 15 February 1964 against the champion of the newly revived junior lightweight division, Flash Elorde, who was stopped in fourteen rounds, the only time that Flash Elorde had ever failed to go the distance. It was now time to accommodate the Michigan State 'world champion' at San Juan, Puerto Rico, 11 April 1964. Ortiz took the play away from Lane with tales of the unexpected, digging so hard to the body – which was Lane's own speciality – that the challenger would be urinating blood for at least a week, and walking away with an undisputed fifteen-round decision. Even Michigan accepted that fact.

According to all accounts, Ortiz neglected his training when he faced equally fast and polished Ismael Laguna in Panama City, 10 April 1965. The champion had seriously under-rated the rapid-fire fists of Laguna. Ortiz confessed:

I still wasn't in shape and I had trouble making the

weight ... I went into the fight like a cripple, like a zombie. So, man, I was feeling real bad. I got my face all bloodied up ... But I'm not taking anything away from Laguna. That kid was fast, I tell you, real fast. *Gee*, I said, *this kid is lightning fast*. He was a whip. The first time I thought I was going to kill him because he was a tall skinny kid. I said, 'I'm gonna kill this guy in 2 rounds. It'll be no contest.' When I got into the ring with him I couldn't see him. He was so fast. I said, *Shit, what's happening here?* Boy, was he fast! And he beat me ... I was disappointed, like everybody should be.

Laguna won by split decision.

The inevitable rematch was in Puerto Rico, 13 November 1965. This time Ortiz had trained rigorously and showed up in immaculate condition. As he reminisced fondly:

When Laguna came out, he saw a different Ortiz for that fight. He didn't see me go into him. He says, *Gee, this is not the same guy I thought I was going to have.* So I made him come to me. He was reaching. I was going under, hitting him right hand to the body, and tremendous left hooks. I won fifteen rounds. I almost killed him there and it was an easy fight and I thought it was going to be a hard fight. It was an easy fight.

Carlos Ortiz won back his crown by unanimous decision.

The champion gave Laguna a return bout at New York's Shea Stadium on 16 August 1967. Although Laguna's speed was once again superlative, Ortiz had seen a technical error:

But I ruined him because I did the opposite from the one in Puerto Rico, I reversed him. I come out in the first round I said, 'When I come out, the first thing he's going to get is a left-right hook combination.' Man, and I threw it. The funny part of it is that they landed. What a right hand I hit him! And, after that, Laguna was no good no more. It was no contest. I outboxed him. I outpunched him. I out-everythinged him. I won fourteen rounds out of fifteen.

Ortiz retained his undisputed title via fifteen-round unanimous decision.

Laguna was hardly the only man over whom Carlos proved his supremacy. Although Nicolino Loche had held him to a draw in Argentina, 1966, the 1967 defence against Laguna had merely been the climax of a year packed with action. The victims had been Johnny Bizarro (KO–12, Pittsburgh, USA, 20 June); former featherweight champion Sugar Ramos (KO–5, Mexico City, 22 October); and junior lightweight champion Flash Elorde once again (KO–14, New York, 22 November); followed by another KO over Sugar Ramos in four rounds, 1 July 1967, prior to the repeated victory over Laguna. On 29 June 1968, Ortiz laid his crown on the line in Santo Domingo against Carlos Teo Cruz.

It was obvious that something was wrong with the champion when Cruz floored Ortiz in the very first round with a right to the jaw. 'I was tired of defending the title so many times and working so hard,' Ortiz said later, 'that when I got there I wasn't in condition at all. So for that fight I was in no shape at all, at all. I took it for granted and that was my worst fight.' Nevertheless, Ortiz rallied and it was a gruelling, hard-fought bout. Referee Zack Clayton voted for Ortiz at the end of fifteen all-action rounds but was outvoted by the two judges. Cruz was the new champion.

Ortiz did not return to the ring, apart from one nondescript bout, until he announced a comeback in December 1971 and proceeded to win ten in a row. This winning streak was finally ended by Scotland's former world lightweight champion Ken Buchanan, who stopped Carlos for the only time in his career, 20 September 1972. Vanity rather than money must have motivated this endeavour, for Carlos had husbanded his winnings quite well. He had owned a nightclub in the Bronx for some years, then diversified, becoming the proprietor of a Bronx liquor store, a chain of dry cleaning establishments in his native Puerto Rico and several apartment blocks in New York. As far as is known, he lives comfortably with his second wife and family in Orangeburg, a comfortable suburb in New York state. One hopes that he brings to his various business enterprises the same acumen with which he graced the ring during his (briefly interrupted) six-year reign.

The reign of Carlos Teo Cruz of the Dominican Republic lacked similar glory. On 18 February 1969, he was halted in the eleventh round by twenty-year-old Mando Ramos of California, at the Veterans Memorial Coliseum, Los Angeles. A wild right by Ramos caused a mean gash over Cruz's left eye in the eighth round and after three examinations, the ringside doctor wisely advised the referee to halt the bout on a technical knockout. Two years after, Cruz died in an air crash.

New champion Ramos had will rather than skill, though he was the youngest man ever to win the lightweight crown. However, if the crouching tactics of the defeated Cruz had baffled him initially, then he had no hope against the come-back of Carlos Ortiz's greatest foe, Panama's Ismael Laguna. Laguna was only a shade less of a boxer than Ortiz and gave Ramos the youngster a severe lesson, causing his eyes to bleed so badly that Ramos's manager rightly called a halt in the ninth-round at the LA Sports Arena, 3 March 1970.

Having regained the crown, Laguna prepared to defend it against Scotland's Ken Buchanan, San Juan, Puerto Rico, 26 September 1970. The Laguna camp did not rate European fighters and figured that Buchanan, just coming off a close decision loss to Spain's European champion Miguel Velasquez, would be an easy mark. This fight was exquisite. Buchanan had defeated thirty opponents prior to his very close loss to Velasquez, but their names were virtually unknown outside Europe. Laguna won the early rounds with a flicking left jab. It was as swift as a snake's tongue and it piled up the points but Buchanan, who could take a punch, noted that it lacked power. As he stated afterwards:

> That gave me heart. My jab, in contrast, was right on target. And it smashed repeatedly into Laguna's head with some venom ... I slipped in several smashing right crosses that made me feel a lot better ... After ten rounds I felt I was just ahead. I continued to exploit Laguna's weakness in defence and kept my jab pumping away furiously. But I was tiring fast.

Laguna bobbed and weaved, damaging Buchanan with short left hooks to the body and chopping rights to the jaw, whilst Buchanan responded with a left jab worthy of Jem Driscoll. The match was even going into the fifteenth and final round, whereupon Buchanan gave his all to pepper Laguna's face and win the lightweight crown by split decision.

Ken Buchanan, born in Edinburgh, Scotland, 1945, was skilful, tough and honest but his experiences of the ring and out of it made him bitter, and one can hardly blame him. Although he had become Scotland's first world lightweight champion, there was no welcoming reception for him in his native Edinburgh. To his cost he learned that he had to deal with a new menace to the Noble Art: the alphabet boys. These were the newly constituted boxing 'authorities': the World Boxing Association (WBA) and the World Boxing Council (WBC). The WBA grew out of the American National Boxing Association (NBA) and developed alliances with one-third of the world's countries involved in the sport. The WBC grew out of the New York Commission (NYC) and developed alliances with two-thirds of the world's nations involved in the sport. Neither organization was part of any government and they were rightly despised by the sporting press generally and the boxing press in particular. This did not stop the alphabet boys from extorting 'sanctioning fees' for title contests, compiling ridiculous ratings and enforcing ludicrous regulations so that promoters and managers friendly to them could benefit. The boxer never did. In an act of everlasting shame, let us not forget, the WBA stripped Muhammad Ali of his heavyweight crown in 1965 for his 'offence' of honouring his contract to a rematch with Sonny Liston.

Can dishonour go further? Yes, it can and it did when the WBC stripped Ismael Laguna of his well-won crown for no reason that any sane person can discern. It ignored the traditionalist wisdom which is that the champion can only lose his title in the ring if he retires or refuses to meet the leading contender within roughly a year. As a result of a contemptible action by the WBC, Ken Buchanan found himself recognized only as the WBA champion, when he should have received undisputed recognition. Unfortunately, the WBC was in the business of promoting unqualified challengers to the undeserved position of number one contender and then stripping the champion of his title for fighting a more legitimate contender instead. Still more unfortunately, the British Boxing Board of Control (BBBC), which was honest enough on its own territory, had chosen the lesser of two evils in affiliating with the WBC and so did not recognize Buchanan as world champion. 'I was the first Briton to win a world lightweight title since Freddie Welsh in 1914,' Buchanan declared indignantly, and he protested to the BBBC. 'That argument, unfortunately,' he observed bitterly, 'had as much effect as a catapult trying to shoot down an Exocet missile.'

Nevertheless, on 7 December, 1970, Madison Square Garden, Buchanan appeared on the Muhammad Ali–Oscar Bonavena card to fight leading contender Donato Paduano, an unbeaten Italian based in Canada. Buchanan tells it best: 'I picked Paduano off with sharp left jabs and rammed home some heavy body shots. I came out unmarked and won the hearts of the highly critical Garden crowd. I also received a standing ovation, an almost unknown reaction at the Garden.'

The BBBC now sent word that it would recognize Buchanan if he could beat one of the two men accepted as top contenders by the WBC, Spain's unbeaten Eduardo Pedro Carrasco or the former undisputed champion conquered by Ismael Laguna, Mexico's Mando Ramos. A match was made with Ramos in Los Angeles. Yet just a few days before this contest, scheduled for 12 February 1971, Ramos pulled out on account of doctors' diagnoses that he had an infection in 'the lower area'. Respected Mexican fighter Ruben Navarro was substituted at short notice. This was a good fight. Navarro started strongly, flooring Buchanan with a light punch that caught him off balance. Buchanan responded with powerful left hooks. In the second round, Navarro went after Buchanan with close body shots and wild right swings: Buchanan responded with neat, strong left jabbing. The referee warned Navarro for his kidney punching in the fourth. Buchanan reminisced:

> Boy, were they annoying ... and painful. In the same round Ruben tried another tactic, grabbing me round the waist and throwing me against the ropes. That stoked up my anger. He got his reward for the rough stuff in the fifth with five consecutive left hooks to the face. After that round I was in control ... game as he was, he had no real answer.

Buchanan was awarded a unanimous decision by margins of 9–4, 9–4 and 9–2. This time Edinburgh gave him the civic reception he deserved.

This champion, whose outspoken views led some wags to call him 'beyond our ken', then delighted his British fans when he met dangerous puncher Carlos Hernandez, former world light-welterweight champion, at Wembley, completely outboxed him and stopped him in the eighth round. Then on 13 September 1971 he gave a return match to Ismael Laguna in Madison Square Garden for a contest that was even better than their first encounter. Laguna started well, raising an ugly swelling beneath Ken's left eye with his rapier-like jab. 'His undoubted athleticism, skill and speed of footwork reaped a handsome reward early on,' Buchanan admitted. By the end of the fourth round, Buchanan was in trouble. Laguna's speed was enabling him to reach through Buchanan's usually impeccable defence, his illegal kidney punching was slowing down Ken's leg speed and raising ugly welts on his back, and the welt beneath Buchanan's eye was so bad that manager Eddie Thomas could only stop that eye from closing by lancing the 'mouse' with a razor. Buchanan came right back, sensing rightly that Laguna could not keep up the pace, and gradually taking control of the contest, to punish his challenger severely. The fourteenth round saw Buchanan send Laguna staggering all over the ring but the Panamanian came back hard and refused to go down. In the fifteenth, a bleeding Buchanan staggered and dazed Laguna but could not put him down. Even so, the Scotsman's grit and eventual dominance had won him a deserved unanimous decision. 'But it was not so easy for Carol,' he said about his wife. 'Dabbing tears from her eyes, she was asked by newsmen for her opinion of the contest. Looking at my injuries she said, "I'm sick." Then she dissolved into a flood of tears.'

Ken Buchanan was rightly voted 'Sportsman of the Year' by the British Sportswriters' Association in 1971, well ahead of another great Scot, Jackie Stewart, world motor-racing champion. However, the WBC still refused to recognize his proven right to the title. Instead it sanctioned a championship contest between Eduardo Pedro Carrasco and Mando Ramos at the Sports Palace, Madrid, 5 November 1971, awarding the 'crown' to Carrasco when Ramos was disqualified after the eleventh round. On 18 February 1972, Ramos avenged this loss by a split decision victory over Carrasco at the Los Angeles Sports Arena, winning WBC recognition. Traditionalists saw these bouts as being nothing more than contests between good contenders.

Ken Buchanan kept busy, easily outpointing Al Ford at Wembley 1972, then knocking out Andries Steyn in Johannesburg, South Africa, three rounds, just one month later. These were merely tune-ups for what would prove to be a real contest for the crown against the great Panamanian, Roberto Duran, the man they called 'Fists of Stone'. There was quite a build-up to this match which took place in Madison Square Garden, 26 June 1972.

It is hardly surprising that 19,000 fans paid $225,000 in live gate receipts alone, not to mention TV revenue, in order to witness this classic contest between a boxer and a fighter. Roberto Duran, who had fought his way out of the slums of Panama City, had never lost a bout in well over twenty-five recorded contests. There was iron in his jaw, in his body and in his will to win. He could punch very hard with either hand and his cunning weaving and bobbing made it very hard to hit him in return. Ken Buchanan, who had fought his way out of the slums of Edinburgh, had only ever lost one close decision in more than forty bouts. His left was immaculate and though his right did not carry an instant knockout shot, it landed with authority. Moreover, the Garden crowd, usually sceptical about British and European boxers, had given Buchanan's skills far more praise than the man ever received in the British Isles. As one hardened New York newspaper reporter declared:

The moves are made with an insolent quickness, and Ken Buchanan stands up straight in the classic position when he fights.

The left jab could be a beam of moonlight that is turned into steel by action. The guy it strikes generally jerks his head as if acid had been flung into his face. The right hand is rapid, but it seldom clogs up people's heads when he nails them.

This is the way old lightweights used to be. They were nimble and deceitful, and they made fighting a graceful effort. This guy is the lightweight champion, and he seems to be a tourist from the past. The lightweights were the elite of the fight racket, and Buchanan borrowed the skills the dead men used. He is a boxer in the obsolete tradition.

There was needle in the build-up, with the odds favouring Buchanan at 8–5. At the weigh-in, Duran said that he was 'going to war' and he meant it. He insulted the champion by suggesting that he was a Gay Liberationist. 'The title will not be taken from me by words,' the dour, moody Scot replied. At the opening bell, Duran stormed inward, using every particle of his body to inflict damage. His tactics appeared to be aided and abetted by referee Johnny LoBianco. Duran's wild right to Buchanan's back caused Ken to slip to the canvas in the opening seconds and, incredibly enough, the referee ruled this foul blow to be a knockdown. Although Buchanan arose to counter with rights to the body and lefts to the head, he later stated that Duran 'won the opening round'.

Duran charged out for the second round, causing Buchanan to recall him as 'the raging bull'. Although the champion hit him with some solid shots, Duran just shrugged as if they didn't matter and also made Buchanan miss. Ken caused Duran to miss in the third, coming back to pepper him at will but failing to slow down this human dynamo. Duran took the fourth with heavy inside body punching, slowing down the speed of Buchanan's legs. Duran sent Buchanan staggering in the sixth with a left hook and right cross but Buchanan came back with a left hook that sent Duran's gum-shield flying away into the crowd. It was all Buchanan in the sixth as he jolted him with a superb left hook, then boxed so slickly that Duran could barely lay a glove on him. The pattern of battle changed in the seventh, when Duran landed a powerful left hook which drew blood from Buchanan's left eye. The following few rounds were all Duran as he mangled and mugged the style of Buchanan. He kept trapping him in corners, cutting down his mobility and throwing leather at every possible piece of exposed flesh. No one who has seen the video can doubt that by the thirteenth round, the fearsome aggression of Roberto Duran had broken through Buchanan's every skilled defence and had wrecked the champion's timing. It was rare to see Buchanan miss so often.

The bell rang for the thirteenth round. Buchanan landed with a fine combination. Roberto shook his sweat from his head and pressed forward with his relentless attack. Towards the end of the round, he forced Buchanan to the ropes and let go an uppercut that landed smack in Buchanan's groin just seconds after the bell. Buchanan collapsed grimacing and clutching his testicles, but managed to arise unassisted and stagger to his corner.

The behaviour of the referee that night was an absolute disgrace to the sport of boxing. No one denies that the champion was trailing on points but it is equally clear that the challenger hit him below the belt. This is a foul and requires either disqualification or severe deduction of points. Furthermore, this foul was committed after the bell to end the round had rung. Reg Gutteridge recalls Buchanan telling his corner, 'I'm hurt,' but he informed the referee that he was willing to continue. The referee should have either disqualified Duran, as would have been done in the much maligned past; or else penalized a foul after the bell by giving the champion a few minutes to recover, scoring it even with the final two rounds to decide the matter, giving perhaps a slight edge to Duran: but he did not. Buchanan was ready and willing to fight on and defend his crown but Johnny LoBianco stopped the fight and awarded it to Duran by TKO. The title went with it.

As if this were not sufficiently deplorable, Roberto Duran, 'The Macho Man', consistently declined all offers to give Ken Buchanan a rematch. The Scotsman's protests were ignored. He told reporters:

All I know is that I was hit low. I was looking into Duran's face so I don't know whether it was a knee or a punch. I told the referee that I was able to come out for the fourteenth round but he refused to listen. I was in agony but I felt as though I could have gone on ... My New York trainer was sure it was twenty-year-old Duran's knee which caused the damage. 'It lifted Ken's protector right up. Only a knee or a hammer could do that,' he said.

The New York Daily News stated: 'Duran was much the better fighter and was well on his way to taking the title away when the incident happened.' Ken Buchanan replied:

I cannot argue with that, nor with any of the scoring. But a foul is a foul and ought not to go unpunished. There were two rounds remaining. Sure I was well behind. But it only takes one punch to turn a fight upside down. In fact I had hit Duran with some of my best punches during the fight and had actually staggered him with a combination just prior to him fouling me.

To their everlasting shame, the Duran camp just didn't want to know about Ken Buchanan any more. Match after match was proposed and bout after bout was declined. It seems unlikely that new champion Roberto Duran was personally guilty of cowardice, but certainly his handlers were.

Buchanan boxed on in the vain hope of a rematch with Duran and performed with credit, winning thirteen straight victories in New York, Miami, Toronto, Copenhagen and Caligari, Italy. On 29 January 1973, at the St Andrew's Sporting Club in Glasgow's Albany Hotel, he fought with all his former skills to beat tough and intelligent fellow-Scot Jim Watt, future WBC world lightweight champion, to take back the British title. Buchanan's superior ring-craft carried the day. 'We both suffered facial damage,' he said, 'but neither of us was ever in any danger of being KO'd.' In May 1974 he outclassed Italian Antonio Paddu to regain the European title and he proceeded to defend it by stopping Leonard Tavarez in fourteen rounds, Paris, 14 December 1974. Since there was no chance of Duran's camp allowing their man into the same ring again with Buchanan, Ken went after the spurious WBC crown, which had passed from Mando Ramos to Erubey (Chango) Carmona (KO–8, Los Angeles, 15 September 1972) to Rodolfo Gonzalez (TKO–12, Los Angeles, 10 November 1972) and to Ishimatsu 'Guts' Suzuki (KO–9, Tokyo, 11 April 1974).

Buchanan now journeyed to Tokyo to face Suzuki, 27 February 1975. He claimed afterwards that a Japanese sparring partner who was a friend of Suzuki had deliberately thumbed his eye in training. Certainly the eye was damaged when Buchanan entered the ring. Even so, the first few rounds were all Buchanan. 'My footwork that night would have been praised by Fred Astaire,' he rightly declared. Suzuki countered by clutching and clinching after every punch he threw. 'I found this extremely difficult to cope with,' said Buchanan. At the end of the fifth, just after the bell rang, Buchanan dropped his guard and as he turned towards his corner, Suzuki threw a right which landed smack on his target, Buchanan's left eye. The Scotsman did not benefit from the referee's warning to Suzuki and was a one-eyed fighter after that. Ken's words were uncharacteristically understated: 'I could not give of my best with only one eye.' Suzuki was awarded a unanimous decision.

There followed a series of 'win some, lose some' contests in various countries against mediocrities whom Buchanan would have wiped away in his prime, but the desire had gone. He was wise to retire to his wife and his Edinburgh hotel. Unfortunately the hotel went bust and his wife left him. He was swindled out of his investments. An ill-advised comeback did not work out and fighting later in unlicensed rings brought only sadness to his fans. Fortunately, you cannot keep a good man down and at the time of writing his autobiography in 1986, Buchanan was once again feeling optimistic as the landlord of a pub, though he remained understandably angry and bitter about the way in which the boxing world had treated his ring wizardry.

Ortiz, Laguna and Buchanan were wonderful boxers who exemplified the most exquisite skills and elegant moves of the lightweight champions at their absolute best. Duran, their successor, would exemplify the incredible ferocity of lightweight champions at their absolute best. Let us not forget, however, that when Duran was asked in 1980 the name of the best man he'd ever fought, he replied without hesitation: 'Buchanan'.

NOTE TO CHAPTER TWELVE

CARLOS ORTIZ
Lightweight champion of the world: 1962–5; 1965–8
World junior welterweight champion: 1959–60.
Total bouts: 70.
Won: 61 (30 by KO, 31 by decision).
Lost: 7, (1 by KO, 6 by decision).
Draws: 1.
No Contest: 1.

ISMAEL LAGUNA
Lightweight champion of the world: 1965; 1970.
Total bouts: 74.
Won: 64 (36 by KO; 28 by decision).
Lost: 9 (KO by 0; 9 by decision).
Draws: 1.

CARLOS TEO CRUZ
Lightweight champion of the world: 1968–9.
Total bouts: 57.
Won: 42 (13 by KO; 29 by decision).
Lost: 13 (2 by KO; 10 by decision; 1 by foul).
Draws: 2.

MANDO RAMOS
Lightweight champion of the world: 1969–70.
WBC lightweight champion 1972.
Total bouts: 49.
Won: 37 (23 by KO; 14 by decision).
Lost: 11 (6 by KO; 4 by decision; 1 by foul).
Draws: 1.

KEN BUCHANAN
Lightweight champion of the world: 1970–2
Total bouts: 68.
Won: 61 (27 by KO; 34 by decision).
Lost: 7 (1 by KO; 6 by decision).
Draws: 0.

WBC TITLISTS

EDUARDO PEDRO CARRASCO
WBC champion: 1971.
Total bouts: 109
Won: 104, (66 by KO; 35 by decision; 3 by foul).
Lost: 3 (0 by KO; 3 by decision).
Draws: 2.

CHANGO CARMONA
  WBC Champion: 1972.
  Total bouts: 66.
  Won: 51 (42 by KO; 9 by decision).
  Lost: 13 (5 by KO; 8 by decision).
  Draws: 2.

RODOLFO GONZALES
  WBC Champion: 1972–4.
  Total bouts: 69.
  Won: 61 (50 by KO; 10 by decision; 1 by foul).
  Lost: 7 (4 by KO; 3 by decision).
  Draws: 1.

ISHATSU 'GUTS' SUZUKI
  WBC Champion: 1974–6
  Total bouts: 51.
  Won: 31 (17 by KO; 14 by decision).
  Lost: 14 (5 by KO: 9 by decision).
  Draws: 6.

13

Fists of Stone

Hard-bitten veterans love to pile into a tough inner city gym and jeer at young hopefuls working out, telling them that they're not a patch on the greats of the past. Only the stupid sneered at young Roberto Duran. Old men with skin like tanned leather watched him spar and whistled through their teeth. Here was one, they thought, who could have mixed it with Gans, Nelson, Leonard, Canzoneri, Ross, Armstrong and Ike Williams. Some observed his imperviousness to punishment and called him 'a miniature Marciano'. The more observant discerned that his weaving and bobbing style made him very difficult to tag solidly and called him a smaller version of Jack Dempsey. The most observant of all perceived that there had never been anyone exactly like him in the ring before.

It is true that he fought as though he wanted to kill his opponents: there was nothing new about that. He hit very hard with either hand, specializing in short, accurate hooks which never gave his enemy a break, and his left hook to the liver was particularly wicked. He used his head, elbows and knees in the clinches. He took an enormous and visible joy in the act of fighting. Whenever he was hit, he laughed, then hit back thrice as hard. All this had been seen before: but Duran was also a highly skilful boxer.

He was born in the worst slums of Guarare, Panama, on 16 June 1951, where he endured a brutal childhood. One of eight children brought up by a deserted mother, he forged his way to the front of a street gang on Faefan beach. His section was named Duran beach. 'Why?' asked a reporter in later years. 'Because anyone come I don't like, I keel them,' Duran responded. Sometimes he swam two miles a day to raid mango trees, coming back through the water with a loaded sack clutched within his teeth. On one occasion, the haul of swag was so big that he nearly drowned. 'Three of us had to grab him and drag him ashore,' said a friend, 'he wouldn't let go of the sack.'

His break came when he was caught stealing coconuts from the estate of Carlos Eleta, an industrialist who also owned an airline and the sole rights to distribute cigarettes in Panama. Eleta liked the look of this boy and persuaded him to turn professional boxer, promising him a better living than he'd had before.

Duran entered the professional ring at the age of sixteen and proceeded to destroy everyone they put in front of him, 1967–72. Prior to fighting for the title, he racked up twenty-eight straight wins, twenty-three by KO, with twelve inside the first three rounds. Carlos Eleta wisely employed veteran trainer Ray Arcel, a rightly acknowledged legend among champions, to hone him in the finer points of pugilism. Top contender Angel Robinson Garcia managed to keep Duran from getting too close to him and went the ten-round distance, but only through running and clutching. We have seen how Duran beat Ken Buchanan to become lightweight champion of the world.

He was called 'The Macho Man' by historian Peter Arnold. Former world light-heavyweight champion turned writer and boxing commissioner, Jose Torres, called Duran the greatest fighter of the decade, pound-for-pound greater even than Muhammad Ali. 'Duran has ring sense,' said Ray Arcel. 'It's an art; a gift from God that flows out of a fighter like a great painting flows out of an artist, or a great book flows out of an author. Ring sense is a natural ability to cope with any situation in a fight. It cannot be taught.' Arcel had also trained the great Benny Leonard. 'I had not seen a more ferocious fighter who lived up to his image of malevolence,' Reg Gutteridge stated, ' ... who always fought with hate in his heart ... Regrettably, I find barely a redeeming feature in Duran, an arrogant, ill-mannered fighter, who frequently made obscene gestures to opponents and always bragged of "killing" them.' 'He's the kind who kept winning in the survival of the fittest,' said Henry Cooper. 'He scowled and fought like an animal.'

The Sixties had witnessed Flower Power, 'Peace and Love', and enticingly beautiful skills among lightweight champions. Now Duran said words to the effect of 'bollocks to that'. He iced Greg Potter and Lupe Ramirez in one round each at Panama City in September and October of 1972. Assistant trainer Freddie Brown was worried nevertheless when his man faced outstanding contender Esteban DeJesus in New York, 17 November 1972, for a non-title fight. Duran was addicted to fatty foods and had difficulty making the weight. 'The only time Duran is serious is when he's sleeping or when he's fighting,' the former cut-man to Rocky Marciano sighed wearily. DeJesus boxed superbly to hand Duran his first loss via ten-round decision and Duran never forgave DeJesus for the insult of flooring him in the first round.

After that loss, Duran whirled back like a human tornado. In an era when there were many notable contenders, he surpassed Joe Brown in defending his crown a record twelve times. From his accession to the throne to his relinquishment,

1972–9, he fought thirty-nine times and won them all, with twenty-nine by KO. 'The guy ranked with the best lightweights in history,' said Angelo Dundee, justly famed trainer of Muhammad Ali, who often worked in the corner of Duran's challengers.

Duran kept looking for a rematch with Esteban DeJesus, thirsting with a passion for vengeance as he powdered all contenders into smithereens. One victim via ten-round KO was Japan's Ishimatsu 'Guts' Suzuki, 8 September 1973, Panama City. As we have seen, Suzuki would go on to win the spurious 'WBC lightweight championship', defending it successfully against Ken Buchanan – and losing it to Esteban DeJesus. On 16 March 1974, Duran put his crown on the line against future claimant DeJesus and proceeded to punish him cruelly. DeJesus, a tough man, offered stiff resistance but was being pulled to bits by the eleventh round. Exhausted by Duran's relentless fury, he sank slowly to the deck from a double left hook to the jaw followed by a right head-hunting smash.

Hardly anybody could stand in the way of Duran. There was a very brave effort made in Panama City, 2 March 1975, by contender Ray Lampkin. He marched right into an undertrained Duran, socked him and staggered him in the fifth, and after ten rounds had him trailing on points. Nevertheless the cold-eyed, hot-hearted Duran came charging back to stop his gallant challenger in the fourteenth. Some observers objected that some blows were low. Duran was indeed one hell of a man but not even his friends would call him a gentleman.

After winning one fight after another, including a notable points victory over the very clever Saoul Mamby, a future junior welterweight champion, Duran was granted his heart's desire in fighting Esteban DeJesus, now WBC lightweight champion, for the *undisputed* title at Caesar's Palace, Las Vegas, 21 January 1978. There was sadistic glee on Duran's face that night. Sometimes a fighter laughs when hit to disguise the fact that he has been hurt, but Duran really meant it; and the punches of DeJesus just gave him extra adrenalin. Having established control with a fast and strong left jab in the early rounds, Roberto proceeded to torture Esteban with vicious and astutely timed body shots. Duran let it go on round after round, totally wrecking DeJesus, who collapsed in the twelfth and lay on the canvas, twitching horribly. Afterwards Roberto laughed like the proverbial drain.

There was nobody left in the lightweight division who might be a credible contender against this extraordinary champion. He might be an unpleasant fellow – 'Sometimes he loves you, sometimes he wants to kill you,' said his trainer Freddie Brown – but nobody at his weight and in his time had a ghost of a chance against him. Duran therefore decided to invade the welterweight division, even though it was going through an exceptionally fine period. Joe Gans and Benny Leonard had both tried and failed at that level. Still, Barney Ross and Henry Armstrong had succeeded. Publicists started beating the drums for there was a major threat to Duran out there in the athletic shape of Olympic gold medalist, Sugar Ray Leonard.

In common with Duran, Leonard was a ring marvel. There the similarity ended. Leonard was always chivalrous to his foes whereas Duran despised them. Duran had had to slug his way out of the slums whilst Leonard turned professional after the Olympics with a lucrative TV contract which earned him more money within a few fights than Duran had earned in his entire career prior to winning the lightweight championship. Leonard looked so pretty and Duran looked so ugly. Although Duran astonished veterans with his unique combination of toughness and skill, Leonard astonished them also with his speed and grace; and his perfectly co-ordinated bodily movements reminded some of a smaller Muhammad Ali. These two were headed for a collision.

Leonard, boxing at the welterweight poundage, proceeded

to beat every man put in front of him with dazzling artistry. In 1979, he stopped leading contender Pete Ranzany; KO'd another, Andy Price, in one round; and then won the WBC claim to the welterweight championship by stopping its outstanding champion, Wilfredo Benitez, with six seconds remaining in the fifteenth and final round. Benitez had been the youngest ever champion at junior welterweight 1976 and after losing the WBC welterweight title, would go on to become junior middleweight champion. He was an exquisitely slick boxer, yet Leonard outslicked him and halted him for the first time yet in this man's most notable career. After that, he defended his share of the crown against England's champion, tough Dave 'Boy' Green, who failed to land a solid punch on Leonard and who was iced unforgettably with a perfect short clip in the fourth round. Leonard closed the year undefeated, with nine straight wins, seven by KO.

For his part, Duran tackled the top welterweight contenders, winning ten-round decisions over top men such as Jimmy Heair, Carlos Palomino and Zeferino Gonzalez. The savage war which won him the victory over Palomino is a classic that can be viewed on video; especially since Palomino had been a worthy welterweight champion 1976–9. At this point, *The New York Herald Tribune* posed two questions – Leonard's ability to take a punch and the mauling that Duran might give him: and Duran's ability to punch as hard as he had done at a higher weight level. Duran scored two knockouts over welterweights in 1980, prior to tackling Leonard.

The fight everyone wanted to see took place in Montreal, 20 June 1980. Duran came into the ring snarling. There were millions at stake. He sneered at Leonard. After all, he had defended his lightweight crown against the top men from the United States, Japan, Australia, Puerto Rico, Mexico, Costa Rica, the Dominican Republic and in places such as Panama City, San José, San Juan, Lake Erie, Los Angeles, Miami, Philadelphia and Las Vegas. Leonard had yet to defend his claim to the crown outside of the United States. Peter Arnold has analysed Duran's previous record succinctly: '... most of his opponents were stopped either very early, demonstrating his belligerence and destructibility, or very late, showing his determination and durability.' Yes: Duran normally rushed his opponent and tried to take him out early. If that didn't work, he took a breather in the middle rounds, tired his opponent – for a man could break his hands hitting him – then came back like a whirlwind to take out a tiring enemy in the latter stages of the fight.

Although the odds favoured Sugar Ray Leonard, Duran was not worried. No lightweight champion had ever matched his record of twelve successful defences, with twenty-four non-title wins, including twenty-nine KOs. As the bell rang, he tore into Sugar Ray, forcing him to back up, and sent him staggering in the second. Leonard refused to fold and swarmed back with accurate two-fisted punching. Duran laughed in his face, forcing Leonard into his greatest error of this remarkable match. Leonard, upset by Duran's taunting and the criticisms of observers who said that this pretty boy could never mix it with Duran, elected to slug it out with his foe. He proved indeed that he could take it and won the respect of the boxing world, but Duran was better at that game than Leonard and proceeded to pile up the points. On the in-fighting, he was out-punching Leonard at a rate of two to one – and Leonard had incredibly fast hands. These extraordinary men slugged it out before over 46,000 paying punters and millions of TV viewers all over the globe.

On a personal note, I switched on the TV that night in my London home, in the company of my then wife, a close male friend and his girl-friend. There was a bet between us men: I was betting Leonard; and partly because he'd seen Duran live in Madison Square Garden, he was betting on Roberto. The women were initially bored by our insistence on watching this contest but became increasingly intrigued. By the sixth round, they were gasping audibly, incredulous at the energy unleashed.

The wife of the champion, Juanita Leonard, was in tears by the third round. The cameras showed her fainting in the eighth. There was no need, for her husband Ray was fighting back with no intention of going down. To an ice-cool observer, Leonard was allowing his toughness to outstrip his intelligence in trying to beat Duran at his own game. The twelfth, for example, witnessed two-fisted fury on both sides and one could only score it even. Duran normally blasted out a man who had lasted that long within the next three rounds. Leonard tried to take the play away from him by redoubling his assault. Duran's body attack gave him the thirteenth and fourteenth but Leonard came back to take the final round: Duran seemed so sure that he'd won the contest, he relaxed throughout it and gave it away. Reg Gutteridge thought that Leonard had won a very close points victory. My friend, betting on Duran, said: 'Leonard' and put his money on the table. I said: 'It's very close. Who knows?' Bert Sugar would later state that in his opinion Duran suckered Leonard into making the wrong sort of fight and giving it to the challenger. The judges gave it to Duran too by unanimous decision. I paid for my lost bet. The women applauded the wonderful bout.

There had to be a return match, and champion Duran gave this to Leonard in New Orleans, 25 November 1980. It proved one of the most controversial in boxing history. It has been said that Duran entered the ring unfit and under-trained that night, having eaten too much steak and ice-cream, but it does not look like that on repeatedly reviewing the video. He looks more than willing and ready to fight, as always. The first couple of rounds were even, then Leonard broke away and began to score points at long-range. Duran found it hard to move inside Leonard's serpentine left-jab. Leonard didn't want to repeat his earlier mistake and so he now outboxed Duran. Duran grew increasingly frustrated and on occasion rushed Leonard to the ropes. Leonard responded with combinations to the head so swift that they baffled Duran, then moved away. This time the matador was beating the bull.

The seventh round was utterly extraordinary. Leonard started to taunt Duran, sticking out his jaw and inviting a punch, then laughing openly whenever Duran missed. The aficionados started laughing too. An enraged Duran failed in his every endeavour to crowd Leonard, who kept jabbing him and mocking him. Duran's charges, in which it was his turn to be out-punched two to one, did no good and made him look increasingly foolish. At one point, Leonard whirled his right around in the air and as Duran stared at that, smashed him with a left hook to the jaw. Duran shrugged off the effect but went back to his corner looking miserable.

The same story was repeated in the eighth. By now, Leonard had his number and was playing with Duran. Ordinary fight fans were joining the aficionados in their laughter. 'Mr Macho' was looking like a clown. Suddenly, Duran astounded one and all by turning to the referee to say: *'No mas. No mas.'* He turned his back on Leonard and walked back to his corner. Leonard jumped in with a powerful right hand hook to Duran's right kidney; a painful blow which could have felled most men. Duran just shrugged his shoulders and walked out of the ring. Leonard had won back his welterweight championship WBC claim by TKO.

The boxing world was stunned. How was it possible that Duran, a man with a jaw of iron, a body of steel, and fists of stone could have quit in the middle of a fight when he was not seriously injured? Various sinister theories were advanced. The answer is relatively simple. Duran could take as much physical pain as any fighter who has ever lived. One could take a machete to cut off his left arm and he would still keep fighting with his right. What he could not take was public ridicule. That was why he quit. 'I don't wreck men's bodies,' said Sugar Ray Leonard, 'I wreck their minds.'

For Duran, the consequences were unfortunate. He had not only lost his title, he had lost universal respect. In his native country of Panama, he had been a national hero. Its president had telephoned him to offer congratulations over his first victory against Leonard. Now a mob came out of the slums and stoned the house Duran had bought his mother. Those who had cheered him now jeered him.

'Failure is not falling down,' said 1920s film star Mary Pickford, 'it is staying down.' Against all odds, Duran essayed a comeback. Everyone was sceptical. Two decision wins against Nino Gonzalez and Luigi Minchillo qualified him for a title shot against Wilfred Benitez, holder of the WBA light/junior middleweight crown. As usual, Benitez boxed superbly that night of 30 January 1982 at Las Vegas. His flicking left never left Roberto's face and it was usually followed by a right cross which had some authority and kept Duran away. No one could quarrel with the unanimous decision in favour of Benitez. Later in the year, Duran boxed England's Kirkland Laing. Laing was an extraordinarily erratic boxer with unusual moves who could look unbeatable on one occasion and utterly inept on the next. He was sharp on the night that he won a decision over Duran in Detroit. A laboured points win over England's Jimmy Batten in Miami did nothing to increase the fallen reputation of Duran.

On 29 January 1983 in Las Vegas, a match was made for the allegedly faded Duran to meet KO artist Pipino Cuevas, former WBA world welterweight champion. Duran slaughtered Cuevas, knocking him out of big-time boxing in the fourth round. This led to a match for the WBA junior middleweight title in New York's Madison Square Garden, 16 June 1983. Duran, a 3–1 underdog, beat Davey Moore into a pulp as Muhammad Ali stood up and cheered for him. One is reminded of the words enunciated in *The World Is Full of Divorced Women* by Jackie Collins, that true greatness in a man is shown, not by winning, but by coming back from a horrible beating to win again.

Even Duran's greatest fans, however, thought that he had bitten off more than he could chew when he challenged

Marvelous Marvin Hagler for the undisputed middleweight championship of the world, 10 November 1983 at Las Vegas. Hagler is one of the greatest fighters ever to have held this crown. He had destroyed all the middleweight contenders in the same way that Duran had destroyed the lightweights, and this at a period when there were many good men fighting hard at that poundage. Seven legitimate challengers, including Great Britain's hard-punching Tony Sibson, had failed to last the distance against Hagler. 'After you've fought Hagler, you're never the same man again,' Alan Minter stated on TV, and he was the accomplished British world champion whom Hagler had pulverized at Wembley to win the crown. However, Duran gave Hagler tough and thrilling defiance. Duran treated Hagler's superior weight and strength with his customary disdain, piling up some points. Hagler looked visibly worried by Duran's experience and tenacity. His punches just seemed to bounce off Duran's thick skull, an unusual experience for him, and his spear-like right cross with which he led, being a southpaw, just kept missing. Nevertheless, Hagler rallied to batter Duran. Duran took it and fought back. By the twelfth round, it was quite a struggle but gradually the middleweight was prevailing over the former lightweight. Although Duran kept punching and went the distance, no one can dispute that Hagler landed a greater volume of effective blows by the end of the fifteenth, and was rightly awarded the unanimous decision. Even so, one could not blame one wag for saying that after this, Marvelous Marvin Hagler should change his name to Semi-Marvelous Marvin Hagler.

Perhaps, though, one sees the truth of ex-champion Alan Minter's words about fighting Hagler if we look at Duran's next important fight on 15 June 1984 at Las Vegas. This was against the great Thomas Hearns. KO artist Hearns had pulverized all opponents on a swift march to the WBA welterweight championship and he was a very good boxer too. He had lost an incredibly fierce contest for the undisputed crown to Sugar Ray Leonard, but recovered to outbox skilful Wilfred Benitez, points winner over Duran, to take his share of the junior middleweight crown (WBC). On this occasion, Hearns gave his greatest performance as 'The Hit Man' and Duran his second worst. It was a stunning KO. Duran, hitherto down only twice in his ring career, fell twice more in the very first round as Hearns unleashed his deadly right hands. In the second, Hearns simply flattened Duran.

Hearns went on to win titles at world level in both the middleweight and light-heavyweight divisions. Duran refused to take this defeat lying down and promptly bounced back to upset all expectations. There is an interesting common factor between these two men in the shape of top contender Iran Barkley. A bloodied Barkley surprised the sporting world by knocking Thomas Hearns through the ropes to take his title in the third round, Las Vegas, 6 June 1988. It was a bigger surprise in Atlantic City, 24 February 1989, when Roberto Duran bulled fearlessly into Iran Barkley. Barkley's powerful left hook sent Duran spinning in the eighth but Duran came storming back to floor Barkley in the eleventh and to win, via split decision, the WBA world middleweight championship. This was an unprecedented accomplishment.

This extraordinary new claimant of the middleweight crown proceeded to defend it against his old enemy, Sugar Ray Leonard. They could match each other when it came to doing things in the ring that had never been done before, including the winning of world championship belts. Duran had won them at lightweight (undisputed) with claims at welterweight, junior/light-middleweight and now middle-weight. Leonard had won his belts at welterweight (undisputed) with claims at junior/light-middleweight, a new division called 'Super-middleweight' and even at light-heavyweight, as had the great rival of both these men, Thomas Hearns. This fight between Duran and Leonard took place in Las Vegas, 7 December 1989. Although millions watched it on TV, the bout was a great disappointment.

Duran appeared to have lost all of the fire that had made him so formidable. Leonard was not as fast as in days of yore and simply boxed at long range, smothering Duran's every assault with clinches whenever the latter tried to come in close. The faint flicking left jab of Leonard won him a just and unanimous twelfth-round decision over the fading Duran, showing that an ageing boxer can usually beat an ageing fighter.

That was Duran's last major contest. He continued to fight, for all the millions he'd earned had somehow been stolen or spent. These days in the ring, he is rather like a policeman: he can beat most of the contenders he faces, though he is physically too old to be of championship standard; and if a young hopeful can get by old, rugged and mean Roberto, there is a future for him. One wishes that Duran could retire with his reputation intact before he starts losing to men he could have wiped away with one swish inside ninety-three seconds during the days of his prime.

Whatever his personal habits and characteristics, he has to be accounted among the greatest of men who ever wore the lightweight crown. Only Gans, Benny Leonard and Ike Williams ever established such awesome supremacy over the division, though Tony Canzoneri, Joe Brown and Carlos Ortiz should also be remembered. Still, none of these men managed to take the welterweight crown from an accepted ring immortal, unless one counts natural welterweights Barney Ross and Henry Armstrong. Even they didn't manage to stake a claim to the middleweight title.

Roberto Duran was an exceptional man and whatever he may do, he remains so. His weaknesses lay in his self-indulgence in matters of under-training and gluttony; and in the fragility of his ego when exposed to public ridicule. His strengths lay in dauntless physical courage accompanied by skills soon appreciated by all who fell victim to them. One may not like him as a man: but one can only admire him as a warrior.

NOTE TO CHAPTER THIRTEEN

ROBERTO DURAN
>   Lightweight champion of the world: 1972–9.
>   Lightweight champion of the world (WBC): 1978–9.
>   Welterweight champion of the world: 1980.
>   Junior middleweight world champion (WBA): 1983.
>   Middleweight champion of the world (WBC): 1989.
>   Total bouts: 85.
>   Won: 78 (59 by KO; 19 by decision).
>   Lost: 7 (1 by KO; 1 by TKO; 5 by decision).
>   Draws: 0.

14

Problems of Succession

Duran, the undisputed lightweight champion of the world, relinquished his crown on 2 February 1979. Unfortunately, the alphabet boys of the WBA and the WBC resolutely refused to co-operate with each other in the best interests of boxing. They held their own tournaments to discover the 'true' champion. Still more unfortunately, TV executives were utterly ignorant of the sport and cared only about viewing figures, allowing the alphabet boys to get away with murder and paying their 'sanctioning fees' for 'world title contests'. Businessmen and more unsavoury persons carried on making money, the boxers continued to be exploited and those who really cared for the sport became increasingly disgruntled.

The WBA version of the world lightweight championship has a worthy but utterly uninspiring history. Ernesto Espana of Venezuela won this 'title' by halting Trinidad's Claude

159

Noel in thirteen rounds at San Juan, 16 June 1979. Espana was then stopped in the ninth by Hilmer Kenty in the Joe Louis Arena, Detroit, 2 March 1980. One year later, 12 April 1981, Sean O'Grady beat Kenty by unanimous decision, Park Place Hotel, Atlantic City. The WBA then withdrew titular recognition from O'Grady for no reason that any sane person can discern. Confusion was added to the matter by a new set of alphabet boys, the World Athletic Association (WAA), which seems to have been formed specifically just to recognize O'Grady. When Andy Ganigan won the spurious 'WAA' title by KO over O'Grady in the second round, Little Rock, Arkansas, both O'Grady and the WAA vanished into a richly deserved obscurity. Not so, alas, the WBA, which recognized Claude Noel as its champion when he won a unanimous decision over Rodolfo 'Gato' Gonzalez, Atlantic City, 12 September 1981. This claim soon passed to Arturio Frias, who flattened Noel in the eighth round, Las Vegas, 5 December 1981, but Frias lost it to Ray 'Boom Boom' Mancini who stopped Frias in the first, Las Vegas, 8 May 1982.

At least Mancini was interesting. He captivated the imagination of the white, blue-collar workers of his own background. His father had been a sound and solid contender a generation before and old men were thrilled when Mancini declared: 'This is for you, dad,' on TV. Mancini was a good fighter with plenty of heart but he couldn't box a lick. He went in wide open, determined to slug toe to toe, taking the shots and giving them back to anyone foolish enough to trade with him; and the crowds loved it. There was never a dull moment once Ray Mancini entered the ring.

Mancini always gave his all and he always bled freely. In nine fights announced as being for a world title, he won five and lost four. His style was simple: non-stop, hard-punching aggression from start to finish: though outside the ring, he had a pleasant personality. His pleasantries did not prevent him from blasting away former WBA champion Ernesto

Espana in six rounds, Warren, Michigan, 24 July 1982. The next defence, however, would be an absolute tragedy.

This disgraceful affair took place in Las Vegas, 13 November 1982 when Mancini defended his claim against Duk-Koo Kim of Korea. Who on earth was Duk-Koo Kim? Nobody really knew. Reputable journals such as *The Ring*, *Boxing Illustrated* and Great Britain's *Boxing News* did not have him figured in their ratings as one worthy of a title shot. Incredibly enough, though, the WBA had Duk-Koo Kim rated as its official number one contender. It is not surprising that Bert Sugar, editor of *Boxing Illustrated*, has called the WBA 'Los Banditos'. Everyone who knows boxing is aware that the WBA ratings bear no relationship to merit whatsoever, and are based upon bribery. This painful truth was displayed to even more painful effect on the night when the innocent Mancini pounded his inept foe so hard that Duk-Koo Kim was stopped in the fourteenth round, fell into a coma and died.

It is the WBA, not Ray Mancini, who must bear the shame and everlasting disgust of those who love the sport for promoting this sordid, squalid event.

Some dignity was restored to the ring on the night Mancini met Peruvian Orlando Ramos, 15 September 1983, New York, and stopped him fairly after nine rounds of fierce fighting. There was an even more strenuous challenge, Reno, Nevada, 14 January 1984 when Mancini faced a man whose heart matched his, Bobby Chacon. Chacon had been the WBC featherweight and junior lightweight champion. In an all-out slug-fest, Mancini stopped Chacon in the third.

Livingstone Bramble took away Mancini's claim to the throne in a tremendous match, in Buffalo, 1 June 1984, winning over Mancini by a fourteenth-round TKO. Mancini could always take a solid punch but his skin cut too easily and Bramble took advantage of the cuts opened above and below his eyes. In their return match, at Reno, Nevada, 16 February 1985, Bramble beat Mancini to the punch all night to take the decision. Although Mancini tried to win the 'junior welterweight title' sponsored by yet another bunch of alphabet boys, called the World Boxing Organization (WBO), he lost on points in twelve rounds to slick Hector 'Macho' Camacho. Actually, Camacho wasn't particularly macho that night of 6 March 1989 at Reno, Nevada. He simply showed Mancini that boxing is the art of hitting without getting hit.

Bramble defended his claim by stopping legitimate contender Tyrone Crawley, Reno, Nevada, 16 February 1986 in the thirteenth. He was a fierce and quick two-fisted fighter but he more than met his match in Edwin Rosario, former WBC lightweight champion, hailing from Puerto Rico. On 26 September 1986, Miami Beach, Florida, Rosario took out Bramble in the second round. He proceeded to a successful defence against tough contender Juan Nazario, but then had to face the great and unbeaten Julio Cesar Chavez, 21 November 1987, Las Vegas. Rosario was a murderous puncher, especially at medium range. Chavez came in at close range, smothering him with short and vicious digs to the body that took away Rosario's leg speed. Rosario was helpless in the eleventh round as Chavez hammered him at will, and the referee rightly called it. Chavez now had seized the WBA title; but what of the WBC lineage?

This was really rather more interesting. On 17 April 1979, Scotsman Jim Watt had won his claim by defeating Alfredo Pituala, halting him in the twelfth round in his native Glasgow. Watt was a very good boxer. Without having one-punch knockout power in either fist, he nevertheless punched with authority and consistently used his brains. Although in his younger days, Watt had lost to more experienced ex-champion Ken Buchanan, he had learned by experience. He jabbed sharply and stiffly, playing all the while upon his opponents' mistakes. He joined the most noble company of men such as Driscoll, Moran, Welsh and Buchanan in winning respect at his weight which resounded throughout the British Isles. It was said, with some truth, that the boxers of the United Kingdom might occasionally win a world championship but that they would always fall apart on the first defence, especially if it were against a man trained in the gyms of America. Jim Watt emulated his great predecessors in telling American gyms that 'It ain't necessarily so.' Tough Roberto Vasquez was in grief when the referee halted the contest, Glasgow, 3 November 1979. Ireland's strong Charlie Nash was stopped easily in four. Many Americans bet on Olympic Champion Howard Davis to make a monkey out of Jim Watt, but Watt reversed that game to hand out a solid fifteen-round beating, Glasgow, 7 June 1980. On 1 November of that year, he faced future WBA championship claimant Sean O'Grady and trounced him, winning by a twelve-round TKO.

'Jim looked after himself as a boxer, training hard and watching his weight,' said Ken Buchanan. 'He was a cagey, crab-like opponent and a man blessed with a tremendous asset – the ability to pace himself properly.' At the same time, Buchanan was characteristically cynical. 'All the bouts were in Glasgow. I wish my fights had been in Scotland. Watt's passionate ringside support must have intimidated any opponent.'

On 20 June 1981, Jim Watt journeyed to London, his opponent being the great Alexis Arguello, a boxer and counter-puncher of surpassing excellence. '(Watt) fought like a tiger in front of his ain folk in Glasgow', Ken Buchanan commented sourly, adding: 'The fire was conspicuous by its absence in London.' Watt had proved himself to be good but that night he had no answers to the swift moves of Arguello, whose fluidity made Watt look so rigid and inflexible. No one could argue with the unanimous decision in favour of Arguello. Watt chose to hang up his gloves, wrote an interesting autobiography called *Watt's My Name* and proceeded to a career as a TV boxing commentator. Personally, I find his inter-round summaries to be outstandingly observant. Judging by letters in the tabloids, many do not share my opinion. One wonders what is disliked more – his Scottish accent or the intelligence of his commentary. In any event, Jim Watt is currently crying all the way to the bank.

Watt was good but Arguello was great. In no less than twenty-two contests at world championship level, this man won nineteen and lost three. Born in Managua, Nicaragua, 19 April 1952, he showed early on that he could take a punch although most of the time he was so slick that he didn't have to do that. Lack of experience led to his first loss in a WBA featherweight title challenge against Ernesto Marcel, fifteen rounds, Panama City, 16 February 1974. Alexis rebounded to face the legendary Ruben Olivares in Los Angeles, 23 November 1974, for another go at the featherweight championship (WBA). Olivares was a spectacular fighter with knockout power in each fist. Most experts count him among the best bantamweights of all time, and he held that crown 1969–70 and 1971–2, going on to win the WBA featherweight championship he was defending against Arguello. Arguello was not fazed by the fact that Olivares had knocked out more than seventy men. He took the hiding Olivares's quick fists gave him in the early rounds and came back eagerly for more, just waiting for his opportunity to put Olivares to sleep with a couple of clever, short, sharp shocks in the thirteenth.

After defending his featherweight claim four times with brilliant boxing against the best contenders, Arguello moved up to junior lightweight. Here he won the WBC version of the crown from a very good fighter, Alfredo Escalera, via thirteenth-round stoppage. This was followed by nine successful defences. He fought terrific whirlwind punchers such as Rafael Limon (TKO–11), Bobby Chacon (TKO–7) Ruben Castillo (TKO–11) in addition to his return with Alfredo Escalera (KO–13). All of these men held titles or were fit to hold them at points in their careers: but Arguello was quite simply the best.

Outside the ring, he was a gentleman. There was nothing

wrong with his manners within the ropes either. He always hit above the belt and kept challenging Roberto Duran, claiming that Duran was afraid of him. As we have seen, Arguello totally outboxed goodly Jim Watt to take the WBC lightweight title. On 3 October 1981, Atlantic City, he took future WBA lightweight champion Ray 'Boom Boom' Mancini to the cleaners and back again, leaving him helpless and with no answer when the referee rightly stopped this one-sided slaughter in the fourteenth. After knocking out Roberto Elizondo, Arguello then stopped James Buscerne before going on to halt 'WAA champion', Andy Ganigan in the fifth with a stunning KO.

These victories made the state of the lightweight championship gratifyingly clear to all traditionalists. The WAA was wiped out. Furthermore, since Ray Mancini was now the 'WBA champion' and he had been swept away by Arguello, Arguello was obviously the true lightweight champion of the world. The boxing press recognized him as such and heaved a massive sigh of relief over the simplicity he had restored to the division, all done with such strength and grace.

Alas, matters were not to remain that simple. Arguello relinquished the crown to go after a fourth title, the junior welterweight championship of the world, held by unbeaten Aaron Prior. Prior reminded many observers of 'Hammering' Henry Armstrong. He never stopped punching. When his opponent weakened, he'd fire in a deadly knockout shot, which led his fans to call him 'The Hawk'. Fighting with the manic intensity of a speed freak, he knocked out everybody put in front of him. A terrific fight took place, Miami, 12 November 1982. In the early rounds, Arguello made a punch-bag out of Prior, but the champion refused to take it lying down and stormed back. Arguello hit Prior with rights to the jaw that would have felled a tree, but Prior just kept coming. In the fourteenth, Prior discerned that Arguello was tiring and unleashed a frightening barrage that left his challenger helpless against the ropes. The return, Las Vegas, 9 September 1983, was equally sensational. This time, Prior's ceaseless battering once again wrecked all the swift moves of Arguello as he marched through the latter's power-punching to win by a tenth-round KO.

Neither man was the same again after these two amazing contests. They both hung up their gloves. Unfortunately, both came to grief in their separate ways. Arguello had all his properties in Nicaragua confiscated by the Sandanista government. Prior put all his ring earnings up his nose. Abuse of cocaine destroyed him.

The retirement of Arguello threw the crown into vacancy. Of course the WBA and WBC did not work together to promote the best interests of the sport, holding their own tournaments and endeavouring to keep their claimants of the championship away from one another. Further confusion was added by the newly formed International Boxing Federation (IBF) which awarded its own titles. The ordinary sporting fan was now faced with a hideous prospect. Whereas previously there had been eight weight divisions with eight champions, the new system, with eight additional 'junior' divisions, provided the headache of sixteen divisions with three 'champions' each, a total of forty-eight; and matters would get worse.

For once, the WBC did not do too badly in sanctioning a championship contest between top contenders Edwin Rosario and Jose Luis Ramirez on 1 May 1983, Puerto Rico. Rosario, a terrific puncher, was unbeaten in twenty-two contests and Mexico's Ramirez had only lost three in eighty bouts. Rosario won by twelfth-round split decision. In two defences at San Juan, this credible 'WBC champion' stopped Arguello victim Roberto Elizondo in the first, then beat up Olympic gold winner Howard Davis to win the decision. However, in a return against Ramirez, San Juan, 3 November 1984, Rosario was handed his first defeat when Ramirez, down in the first and second rounds, slugged him to a helpless standstill in the fourth. As we have seen, Rosario would come back to win the WBA version of the title in 1986.

The reign of Ramirez did not last long. In his first defence, Las Vegas, 10 August 1985, he was absolutely outboxed over the twelve-round distance by the astonishing Hector Camacho of Puerto Rico. Camacho, who was a very pretty boy, liked to enter the ring wearing leopard-skin trunks and roar, 'It's macho time!' He would then proceed to use his speed in avoiding his opponents' every punch. It was virtually impossible to tag him solidly. He did not have one-punch KO power but he did have shattering combinations and sizzling ring wizardy in addition to the courage that enabled him to meet the best men of his time.

Camacho had beaten rugged Rafael 'Bazooka' Limon to win the WBC junior lightweight crown, (TKO–5), and had defended it against a legitimate contender, Rafael Solis (KO–5). As WBC lightweight champion, he fought ex-champ Edwin Rosario in New York, 13 June 1986, foxing Rosario's every endeavour to land a solid punch and dancing away with a deserved decision. The next challenger, Uganda's Cornelius Boza-Edwards, was a match for any man. He was an extremely exciting fighter who delighted the crowds with his all-action style, gladly taking three to land one of his sweeping and devastating hooks. He had been the WBC world junior lightweight champion 1981. This match, Miami, 26 September 1986, turned out to be a masterpiece of boxing. Boza-Edwards always came to war and prided himself on his ability to soak up any amount of punishment. How he loved it if a man elected to punch toe-to-toe with him in the ring! Camacho did not make that mistake. He refused to meet the commendable Boza-Edwards on the latter's own terms. Either he stepped out of those deadly hooks or he stepped inside them. Boza-Edwards had no answer to Camacho's speed, amazing reflexes and accurate counter-punching. Camacho won a merited decision, then announced that weight difficulties were sendng him onward and upward towards the junior welterweight title.

Here his career disappointed even his greatest fans, which was unfortunate in one so naturally talented. He won a version of the junior welterweight championship according to some recently formulated bunch of alphabet boys, the WBO. He defended and retained this spurious claim successfully against former WBA lightweight title claimant Ray Mancini, Vinnie 'The Devil' Pazienza and Tony Balthazar (all in twelve). Tough Greg Haugen took his claim away, crowding him to win via decision, but lost it back the same way. What had happened to Camacho, who had laboured uninspiringly? An excess of junk food? An abuse of illegal or legal substances? A moment of truth came when he faced the great Julio Cesar Chavez, subject of a future chapter, in Las Vegas, 12 September 1992. Chavez just charged through all the defences of Camacho, causing him to clutch and run. This bout was for the WBC junior welterweight title, which had rather more world-wide credibility than that of the WBO: and champion Chavez had rather more credibility than challenger Camacho. Chavez cut the ring, slowed down Camacho's mobility and punished him severely. To his credit, Camacho showed that he could take it and finished the fight wobbly but still on his feet, losing a unanimous decision with which nobody argued. It is not known where Camacho will go from there.

Meanwhile, Jose Luis Ramirez, former WBC champ, had stormed back to take that crown again with a marvellous two-fisted win over strong Terrence Alli in St Tropez, France, 19 July 1987. He proceeded to prove what a worthy fighter he was by knocking out fierce Cornelius Boza-Edwards in the fifth, then giving a lesson to future great champion Pernell Whitaker via twelve-round decision. Finally and at last – and about time too – this WBC champion was matched with the WBA champion, Julio Cesar Chavez, Las Legas, 29 October 1988. Ramirez was his customary brave and proficient self but he simply couldn't cope with being out-punched three to one by Chavez. Chavez was way ahead on points when an accidental butt forced a halt in a ring covered with blood. WBC rules dictate that, under these circumstances, the decision must be awarded to the boxer who is ahead on the judges' cards at the time of the stoppage, and this was clearly Chavez. Traditionalists promptly recognized Chavez as *the* lightweight champion of the world.

The IBF appeared to have no interest in common sense. In 1984, it had recognized as champion Charley 'Choo Choo' Brown on account of his split decision win over Melvin Paul. Three months later, Harry Arroyo halted Brown in the fourteenth, only to lose it via unanimous fifteen-round decision to Jimmy Paul a year later. These three bouts took place in that paradise for gamblers, Atlantic City. Then, at the rival gamblers' Mecca, Las Vegas, rough Greg Haugen beat Jimmy Paul via split decision. Wily Vinnie Pazienza, whose heart matched his ring cunning, decisioned Haugen in 1987 but Haugen bulled his way back in the following year to retake his claim via decision in Atlantic City.

As if the IBF were not being sufficiently tedious in awarding fake 'championships' to otherwise solid and respectable contenders, the WBO chose to add its own extra element of boredom to the matter. Few had heard of Maurico Aceves and Amancio Castro. Nevertheless these men were matched for something called 'the WBO lightweight championship of the world', 20 January 1989, in Monteria, Columbia. They boxed a draw.

Traditionalists ignored this nonsense. As far as aficionados were concerned, the true champion of the lightweights was Julio Cesar Chavez, who had won both the WBC and WBA claims and who had gone an incredible fifty-five fights without one loss. In a manner reminiscent of Roberto Duran, he didn't merely beat his opponents, he totally destroyed them. One wondered if there was anybody out there who could give Chavez anything more than a ghost of a challenge.

On 18 February 1989, Virginia, Pernell Whitaker won IBF recognition as 'champion' by outpointing Greg Haugen. So far, so uninteresting – yet he displayed an astounding mastery of pugilistic skills, showing just how much he'd learned from his close loss to Jose Luis Ramirez. Whitaker would go on to decision Ramirez to take the WBC title in 1989 and would win the WBA title in 1990.

The supporters of Chavez and Whitaker argued that their own champion was unbeatable. Everyone involved in sport wanted to see this match. Questions remained as to where, when, at what weight, for which title(s) and before what judges?

NOTE TO CHAPTER FOURTEEN

The present writer's love of the Noble Art and hatred for those who despoil it are assuredly evident. In consequence, only the ring records of those recognized as champions by traditionalists are supplied; though I append lists of the 'titles' as enumerated by the alphabet boys.

JIM WATT
Lightweight champion of the world: 1981.
WBC lightweight champion of the world: 1979–81.
Total bouts: 46.
Won: 39. (28 by KO; 11 by decision).
Lost: 7 (2 by KO; 5 by decision).
Draws: 0.

ALEXIS ARGUELLO
Lightweight champion of the world: 1982–3.
WBC lightweight champion of the world: 1981–3.
WBA world featherweight champion: 1974–7.
WBC world junior lightweight champion 1978–80.
Total bouts: 83.
Won: 77 (63 by KO: 14 by decision).
Lost: 6 (3 by KO: 6 by decision).
Draws: 0.

WBC CHAMPIONS

Jim Watt 1979–81.
Alexis Arguello 1981–3 (relinquished title).
Edwin Rosario 1983–4.
Jose Luis Ramirez 1984–5.
Hector Camacho 1985–7 (relinquished title).
Jose Luis Ramirez 1987–8.
Julio Cesar Chavez 1988–9 (relinquished title).

WBA CHAMPIONS

Ernesto Espana 1979–80.
Hilmer Kenty 1980–1.
Sean O'Grady 1981.
Claude Noel 1981.
Artruro Frias 1981–2.
Ray Mancini 1982–4.
Livingstone Bramble 1984–6.
Edwin Rosario 1986–7.
Julio Cesar Chavez 1987–9 (relinquished title).

IBF CHAMPIONS

Charley 'Choo Choo' Brown 1984.
Harry Arroyo 1984–5.
Jimmy Paul 1985–6.
Greg Haugen 1986–7.
Vinny Pazienza 1987–8.
Greg Haugen 1988–9.
Pernell Whitaker 1989–92 (relinquished title).

WBO and WAA claimants can be ignored with impunity.

15

Ears and Tail

There can be no doubt whatsoever that in 1987–9, Julio Cesar Chavez was the greatest lightweight in the world, and forging fast towards a place among the greatest lightweights of all time. Spaniards and Mexicans, devotees of bullfighting, customarily award the ears and tail of the slain bull to the victorious matador. The greatness of Chavez resides in the fact that he could be both matador and bull, switching from one role to another with bewildering rapidity.

Inside the ring, Chavez was a killer. He didn't actually want to murder his opponents: but he did want to destroy them. Bert Sugar called him 'the most economical and efficient puncher in the last thirty years ... (with) an almost superhuman ability to take a punch'. Outside the ring, he was a pleasant man, gracious and gentle in his manners.

This all-time ring great was born on 12 July 1962, one of ten children in Ciudad Obregon, Mexico. It was as though

God had made him to fight as he charged straight through one opponent after another. He could box with boxers and slug with sluggers, although he sometimes elected to box a slugger or slug a boxer. One of the most intriguing matters about watching Chavez was that every round was unpredictable. It was hard to understand him, for he said few words before a fight. If he talked at all, it was afterwards, when his words were short and to the point, as were his punches.

For an undeservedly long time, the reputation of Chavez was confined to Mexico's tough rings. Here he fought good men for not much pay but he beat everybody. A chance to take the matter further came when he stopped Mario Martinez, Los Angeles, 13 September 1984, to take the WBC junior lightweight title. He followed this with nine successful defences against very fine fighters. These included Roger Mayweather, WBA junior lightweight champion 1983–4 and WBC junior welterweight champion 1987–9. This man won eight and lost four bouts for the world title but Chavez halted him in two for his WBC junior lightweight defence, 7 July 1985, Las Vegas; and would later powder him in ten to take his WBC junior welterweight title, Los Angeles, 13 May 1989. Veteran Raul Rojas, former WBA featherweight champion, was rendered helpless in the seventh round. Rocky Lockridge, WBA junior lightweight champion 1984–15, lost the twelve-round decision to Chavez in Monte Carlo, 3 August 1986, though he went on to win the IBF junior lightweight title 1987–8. That very fine WBC featherweight champion Juan LaPorte, (1982–4), was clearly outpointed in New York, 12 December 1986. Having established himself as being the greatest of the junior lightweights – also called the super-featherweights – Chavez mounted his challenge for the lightweight crown.

As we have seen, he beat Edwin Rosario to win the WBA title, then, after slaughtering Rodolfo Aguila (TKO–6) in its defence, he beat tough Jose Luis Ramirez on a technical decision to take the unified lightweight championship of the world. Fernando Paramo, sports editor of *La Opinion*, said:

The only time I have seen him on a slower pace was against Jose Luis Ramirez, and that was because apparently he had something wrong with his ribs. I have seen him fight with bad hands when he fought Cabrera in Tijuana. I have seen him fight with a knotted stomach when he fought one of the guys from Panama (Rodolfo Aguila) in Vegas ... When he fought Adrian Arreola in LA, he had diarrhea. So you look at a fighter that, regardless of how he is, he still gives you a tremendous showing. He has been considered for a while now the best Mexican fighter ever. There has been no other fighter that reigned so long, that has been undefeated so long.

Only bantamweight Ruben Olivares and featherweight Salvador Sanchez can compare with Chavez when Mexican champions are discussed. Legendary trainer Louie Jauregui declared: 'Chavez don't have any weaknesses. He takes a good punch, and he looks awkward to hit, and he's got that inside hook, right hook. Instead of shooting a straight right, he hooks it like he's throwing a ball.'

Chavez was now having difficulties in making the weight and so he vacated his throne to take the WBC junior welterweight title from Roger Mayweather (TKO–10). After defences against Sammy Fuentes (TKO–10) and Alberto Cortes (KO–3), he faced the formidable Meldrick Taylor in Las Vegas, 17 March 1990.

If anyone had a decent chance against Chavez at that time, it was Taylor. This dangerous boxer-fighter had won the IBF junior welterweight title from that fine professional, James Buddy McGirt, in 1988 and no man had ever beaten him. The fight was sensational. No one had ever stood up to Chavez like that before. At times, Taylor outpunched him two to one in close exchanges and left Chavez looking puzzled. It took more than that to discourage Chavez, however, and he charged back to try to take the heart out of Taylor. One could only gasp at the incredible energy of these fighters and it was a difficult bout to score. There was a good referee, Richard Steele, yet he did nothing to stop Taylor's repeatedly low blows to Chavez. Going into the twelfth and final round, opinions varied. Judge Chuck Giampa had Chavez ahead by one round and Earl Gustley of the *Los Angeles Times* concurred. I had Taylor ahead by one round and so did the other two judges. To me it looked as though Chavez was being outboxed, although Taylor's punches were doing little damage and those that Chavez landed were making Taylor swallow his own blood. Chavez went hunting in that final round, pinned Taylor against the ropes and unleashed an assault sufficient to injure permanently any man in good health. Just as one was praying that Taylor wouldn't die, the referee intervened and stopped the contest, awarding it to Chavez by TKO. There were only two seconds to go.

The referee's action was widely criticized and the matter is open to debate; but if I had been the referee, I would have done the same thing. It is the referee's job to stop the fight if there is danger of permanent injury or death, without thought for precise time-keeping, and Taylor was at that point helpless before the thunderous fists of Chavez. Afterwards, Chavez drank champagne. Taylor vomited repeatedly and had to go to hospital with severe bleeding from both kidneys and a fracture of his left eye socket. Honestly, who won that fight?

Although Taylor won the WBA welterweight title on points in 1991 and defended it via points wins twice, he was never really the same fighter again and lost his claim in London, 1992, to a virtual unknown, Crisanto Espana (TKO–8).

Chavez carried on winning as though nothing untoward had occurred. There was a particularly notable win over 'Lightning' Lonnie Smith, Las Vegas, 14 September 1991, by unanimous decision. Smith had enjoyed a brief reign as WBC junior welterweight champion, taking this title from Billy Costello with a dazzling display of ring artistry that left even the hardest of veterans open-mouthed with admiration, though he disappointed one and all by walking into a Rene Arredondo KO sucker punch just nine months later. Nevertheless, Smith was on form the night he met Chavez and his superior leg speed won him a few rounds. Chavez responded by never giving him a breathing space, pounding him hard to the body and in the later rounds, going head-hunting. When the decision in favour of Chavez was announced, Lonnie Smith looked relieved just to have gone the distance.

After wins over Angel Hernandez (TKO–5) and Frank Mitchell (TKO–4), Chavez handed out a sound beating to Hector 'Macho' Camacho (W–12). By December 1993, Chavez had performed at levels unsurpassed by any boxer in the entire history of the sport. Now he held the WBC super lightweight (junior welterweight) title, having already held the titles at WBC super featherweight (junior lightweight); the WBA, WBC and traditionalist lightweight championship of the world; and the IBF junior welterweight title. He had an incredible record of eighty-five bouts, eighty-five wins, seventy-three by KO. No fighter in boxing history has ever matched that. Outside the ring, he womanized quietly, yet in all other respects was a fine example to youth. After his grubby beginnings in Mexico bar-rooms, he had become an international super-star. When he fought now, his purses were in the millions and his fights were watched all over the globe. He drove visiting reporters to distraction because he declined to say very much, yet his mass appeal was enormous. Another record was broken on 20 February 1993 at Mexico City's Estadio Azteca, when more than 132,274 fans paid at the gate to see him live, going past the 120,000 attendance for Gene Tunney v Jack Dempsey sixty-six years earlier.

His opponent was strong Greg Haugen, IBF lightweight champion 1986–7 and 1988–9, also WBO junior welterweight champion 1991. He had swopped decisions with men of the calibre of Vinny 'The Devil' Pazienza and Hector 'Macho' Camacho. Haugen was unimpressed by Chavez. 'Half the guys he fought,' said Haugen, 'are Tijuana taxi drivers. My Mom could've knocked 'em out. I'm gonna rough him up. Nobody does that. I'm gonna make him respect me. I'm the strongest guy he's ever fought. I've seen him get hit a lot lately. He took a pretty good shellacking from Meldrick Taylor. I'll be right there in front of him, pushing him around, roughing him up.'

'I can walk into the ring drunk and still beat you,' said Chavez. 'Greg Haugen is the only fighter I really dislike … he has always spoken badly of me. I'm not going to knock him out. I'm going to give him the beating of his life … When the opening bell rings, they get the sickness of the running disease.'

Twenty-five thousand people turned out to see Chavez exhibit a public work routine, including Mexico's president, Carlos Salinas de Gotari. Julio Cesar promised his president that the fight would not last the distance. This promise was kept. An immaculately straight right in the first sent Haugen on his first journey to the canvas. After that, Chavez just thrashed him. In the fifth round, Chavez landed twenty-three solid punches without any answer and referee Joey Cortez rightly stopped this uneven slaughter.

Around this time – horror of horrors! – boxing historians Dick Mastro and Dean Lochic discovered that the record of Chavez was not quite as immaculate as previously supposed. Apparently, in his younger days, Chavez had been disqualified against Miguel Ruiz, though the local boxing commission had later reversed the verdict and called it a Chavez win by TKO. No one other than statisticians really cared about this discovery. Nor did Chavez, who proceeded to pound out leading contender, Terrence Alli. But now a real threat appeared in the form of Pernell 'Sweet Pea' Whitaker.

It was rare to see such extraordinarily smooth moves on a man in the boxing ring. Whitaker, born in Norfolk, Virginia, 2 January 1964, had been the 1984 gold medal winner at the Olympic Games. His professional record was remarkable.

After brushing aside all his opponents as though they were a passing irrelevance, he came a cropper against that tough and experienced veteran, Jose Luis Ramirez, and lost a close and controversial decision. That was his only loss. He came back in fine form to win the decision and the IBF lightweight title off Greg Haugen, Hampton, Virginia, 20 February 1989. After stopping Louie Lomeli (TKO–3), he decisioned his old conqueror, Jose Luis Ramirez (W–12), then scored notable victories. The Ramirez win had given Whitaker the WBC/IBF claim to the lightweight championship, and the majority of traditionalists regarded him as being the king. He decisioned Freddie Pendleton, then met dangerous Azumah Nelson of Ghana on 19 May 1990 in Las Vegas. Nelson was one of the greatest featherweight champions of all time. His moves were savagely swift and he could cold-cock a man with either hand. He had held the WBC featherweight championship 1984–7, then he had taken the WBC super featherweight/junior lightweight title 1987–90. Pernell Whitaker wasn't fazed by Nelson's deadly swinging and boxed with scintillating science to take the decision.

The magnitude of Whitaker's victory is shown by the fact that Azumah Nelson continued to defend his 130 pound WBC junior lightweight/super featherweight crown against all comers and is still recognized by traditionalists as champion at the time of writing (1994).

'Sweet Pea' Whitaker, he of the sizzling hand speed, now proceeded to unify the world lightweight championship beyond all dispute. At Lake Tahoe, Nevada, 11 August 1990, he flattened Juan Nazario in just one round to add the WBA belt to his already sufficiently illustrious laurels. This crown was then defended nobly on points against top challengers Anthony Jones, Poli Diaz and Jorge Paez. Whitaker's admirers said that they'd never seen such extraordinary skill. His enemies retorted that he couldn't punch and that a real fighter like Chavez would destroy him. Pernell responded with a cool, calm and collected decision win over Rafael

Pineda to take the IBF world junior welterweight championship.

By this time, even hard and critical experts such as Bert Sugar were comparing him to the immortal Willie Pep. The great debate was whether Chavez or Whitaker was the greatest pound-for-pound fighter of the Nineties. Obviously there had to be a match and this took place at Mexico City's San Antonio Alamodome, 9 October 1993.

Chavez was thirty, with eighty-two wins and no losses; seventy KOs. Whitaker had won twenty-nine with one questionable decision loss and had thirteen KOs to his credit. Both men looked good and talked well before the fight. They were both handsome and articulate in their separate ways. Said Whitaker:

> I don't see any slips in him. I just don't see nobody else putting that pressure on him. He hasn't fought nobody who's gonna make him miss and then make him pay. All he's doing is making other guys pay. But that's a lazy style he has and I'm gonna spice him up. I think hitting him around the body will definitely put some toll on him. A lot of guys may be looking for that one big shot, but I don't look for one shot because I like putting them together ... I won't be there for Chavez to hit. I'm not going to make it a war, I'm going to put on a boxing exhibition. I'm gonna showboat. I'm gonna entertain. I'm gonna use these legs and movement. I'll be in front of him, daring him to punch.

Chavez responded:

> I want to fight Whitaker to remove doubt in anyone's mind. Am I worried about Whitaker? Me? Please! This won't be a hard fight. Whitaker is no good. He can say all he wants to say, but he doesn't scare me. He'll have to fight against me. I will not play with him. I feel very strong about myself.

Chavez's victim Hector Camacho, title claimant at three weights, was in no doubt about the outcome: 'I couldn't keep him off me,' he said of Chavez. 'This is the first time I fought a guy with that much courage ... the pressure he put on me was amazing.'

Some thought that Whitaker's extraordinary ring antics would be his downfall. Against Alfredo Layne, he had jumped in the air, spun around and hit him on the jaw. *En route* to beating top contender Roger Mayweather, Whitaker had pulled his trunks down to his knees. His favourite move came from the legendary Willie Pep, whereby he slipped a punch, ducked down, stepped around and smacked his opponent on the butt. 'People pay good money to come see me fight,' Whitaker retorted. 'I feel I owe it to them to put on a show. One thing they know for sure: they come to see Sweetpea, they get their money's worth.'

More than 56,000 people paid to see this fight live, making it the tenth greatest drawing card in boxing history. Millions more saw it on TV, closed-circuit TV, cable TV or satellite TV, making it one of the richest bonanzas in the history of the sport. It was confirmation of the view that on TV, it is hard to tell the difference between small men and big men – and the viewers don't really care as long as the fight is good.

It turned out to be a good fight with a bad conclusion. Roared on by at least 40,000 live supporters, Chavez charged into Whitaker, taking the opening rounds with his customary ceaseless aggression. Whitaker's trainer, former middleweight contender George Benton, who had done so much for so many boxers, told Whitaker that he was 'fighting in the wrong gear' and urged him to jab and move. Whitaker was wise in taking this advice. One, two, three and four jabs shot into Chavez's face every time he came bulling forward. There was a further surprise when Whitaker, so slender and scrawny, started to outmuscle Chavez in the clinches. Chavez fought back with strong right hand leads to take the fifth but these simply couldn't find the crouching Whitaker in the sixth. A frustrated Chavez took to hitting Whitaker in the thighs so as to ruin his superior leg speed. Whitaker retaliated with a blatant foul to the crotch of Chavez. Referee Joey Cortez wisely ordered a break.

From the seventh to the tenth round, Whitaker took charge. He started to hit Chavez from every angle and Chavez just couldn't land a solid blow on him. It was hard to believe but it was true. 'Pernell Whitaker did for boxing what Degas did for ballerinas, what Van Gogh did for sunflowers, what Warhol did for soup cans,' wrote Bert Randolph Sugar. 'He laid layer after layer of his masterpiece on the canvas ... and proved he was one of the greatest artists in boxing history.'

Ringsiders were aghast in the closing rounds as Whitaker took the fight to Chavez, forcing him to look ungainly and back up. Chavez grew increasingly frustrated but could do nothing about it. He punched air and Whitaker punched him. Bert Sugar commented that Whitaker was successful in expanding the ring whilst Chavez was unsuccessful in contracting it. The rabid supporters of Chavez fell into a subdued silence. It was obvious that on this occasion, the boxer had defeated the fighter with wonderful ring wizardry and even the greatest supporters of Chavez accepted that the decision would be merely a sad formality.

Of course, we had all reckoned without the influence of promoter Don King, for Chavez was firmly established in the stables of his fighters and Whitaker was not. Judge Woodruff gave the fight to Whitaker 115–113; but Judges Marti and Vann ruled it a draw at 115–115. That meant that the final result was a technical draw. The decision stank to high heaven. 'DON'T BUY THIS MAGAZINE IF YOU THINK "THE FIGHT" WAS A DRAW,' shouted the front page of *Boxing Illustrated*, December 1993. I entirely agree.

Julio Cesar Chavez was never the same fighter after that. Following a victory over some over-hyped nonentity, he lost his junior welterweight championship to solid but uninspiring Frankie Randall. Though he may well carry on fighting, it is obvious that the days of his greatest glories are behind him. By contrast, Pernell Whitaker has beaten the outstanding contender, Buddy McGirt, to take not only the WBC welterweight title, but to win also the recognition of traditionalists as the 147 pound champion in a move led by *Boxing Illustrated*, that publication of immaculate integrity.

It is a pity that money and politics soured the decision between Whitaker and Chavez. However, no one can deny that they rank among the greatest lightweights who ever lived.

NOTE TO CHAPTER FIFTEEN

JULIO CESAR CHAVEZ

Lightweight champion of the world: 1988.
WBC lightweight champion: 1988–9 (relinquished title).
WBA lightweight champion: 1987–9 (relinquished title).
WBC junior lightweight champion: 1984–7 (relinquished title).
WBC junior welterweight champion: 1989–94.
IBF junior welterweight champion 1990–1 (title confiscated).
Total bouts: 90.
Won: 88 (73 by KO; 18 by decision).
Lost: 1 (0 by KO; 1 by decision).
Draws: 1.

PERNELL WHITAKER

Lightweight champion of the world: 1990–2 (relinquished title).
IBF lightweight champion: 1989–92 (relinquished title).
WBC lightweight champion: 1989–92 (relinquished title).
WBA lightweight champion: 1990–2 (relinquished title).

IBF junior welterweight champion: 1992–3 (relinquished title).
Welterweight champion of the world (also WBC) 1993–present
Total bouts: 34.
Won: 32 (15 by KO; 17 by decision).
Lost: 1 (0 by KO; 1 by decision).
Draws: 1.

SECOND NOTE TO CHAPTER FIFTEEN

Since the writing of the foregoing, Julio Cesar Chavez has lost and won back his WBC junior welterweight crown under most controversial circumstances on each occasion.

On 29 January 1994 at Las Vegas, virtually one and all agreed that he had been soundly beaten over twelve rounds by unheralded 16–1 underdog, Frankie Randall. Referee Richard Steele, whom some have accused of favouring Chavez in the controversial stoppage over Meldrick Taylor, nevertheless deducted two points for low blows from the champion. Judges Chuck Giampa and Angel Luis Guzman scored it in favour of the challenger at margins of 116–111 and 114–113 respectively. Pat Putnam of *Sports Illustrated* had Randall 114–111 winner as did 'Fast' Eddie Shuyler of Associated Press. It was quite incredible, therefore, that judge Abraham Chavarria of Chavez's native Mexico scored Chavez a 114–113 winner despite an eleventh round in which Chavez was knocked down for the first time in his ring career. The TV microphones picked up on promoter/manager Don King saying, 'Not this time, Julio.' 'Fuck you, Don King,' Chavez replied. He said the same to Richard Steele, the referee, and added extra obscenities. Rarely has a man lost his title with less dignity than on this occasion. He really did disgrace himself. Wallace Matthews called the press conference of

Chavez, 'his own personal finger-pointing, tantrum-throwing hissy fit. It was another sad chapter for a man who has been a champion in the ring and a chump outside it.' *Boxing Illustrated* lamented 'FROM WINNER TO WHINER'.

Another Don King promotion, Las Vegas, 7 May 1994, saw his fighter Chavez regain his title from Randall. An accidental head-butt in the eighth round opened a cut over the eye of Chavez. Under WBC rules – and this is an organization alleged to be dominated by Don King – a point was deducted from Randall's score and this was enough to give Chavez a split decision victory. One wishes that this great fighter would retire, rather than win in this way.

16

'Lightweights,
My Lightweights, Where
Have You Gone?'

The above quotation from a boxing publication of the 1950s aptly sums up the present situation in the division. Admittedly, Chavez and Whitaker were a tough act to follow but nobody has come close to them since that time. The alphabet boys have not assisted matters. A titular champion might have a match made with a top contender only to find that he will be stripped of his 'championship' unless he fights some nobody bribed into a top contender's place. Statisticians and historians are thrown into despair by this appalling situation: and so are the boxers. Unscrupulous promoters and managers continue to make money out of the fighters' blood, sweat and tears. Television networks don't care as long as the result is good sporting entertainment with high viewing ratings. TV commentators have to bite their own tongues if they wish to continue earning a good living. Mr and Mrs Joe and Josephine Q Public haven't a clue about what is really being dished out to them, just so long as it's a good punch-up.

Of course there are some good lightweight boxers out there but none of them have any charisma at present. Who has ever heard of Mauricio Acevez? He won something called the WBO world lightweight championship by outpointing one Amancio Castro in twelve rounds, Santa Ana, California, 6 May 1989 and he lost it via split decision to a Dingaan Thobela at no less a place than the International Convention Centre, Brownsville, Texas, 22 September 1990. As a character portrayed unforgettably by Michael Caine in a forgettable film said: 'Not a lot of people know that.'

The ratings of the alphabet boys are no guide to anything other than the amount of money and pull various managers and promoters enjoy. One turns, therefore, to the rigorously honest *Boxing News* of Great Britain, or else Bert Sugar's *Boxing Illustrated*, in which the ratings are compiled by a worldwide panel of forty experts: and we fail to find Mauricio Acevez, Amancio Castro, Dingaan Thobela, nor any information as to why Thobela relinquished his 'WBO title'. One can only respond, along with true aficionados, with scorn and boredom to learn that Giovanni Parisi won the vacated WBO crown with a tenth-round TKO over Javier Altamirano, Voghera, Italy, 25 September 1992. How thrilling!

For once the WBA had some credibility when former hard-punching champion Edwin Rosario stopped solid contender Anthony Jones in the sixth round, Atlantic City, 9 July 1989. Juan Nazario halted Rosario in the eighth, Madison Square Garden, 6 April 1990, only to be flattened in the first by Pernell Whitaker, 11 August 1990. When Whitaker vacated the crown, the issue of his successor was decided amidst the elegance of the Cumberland County Civic

Center, Portland, Maine, 13 June 1992, when Joey Gamache TKO'd one Chil Sung Chun in the eighth. At the same exciting place, 24 October 1992, Tony Lopez took the title from Gamache by eleventh-round TKO. Action shifted to South Africa, where former WBO claimant, Dingaan Thobela, won the WBA claim with a unanimous decision over Lopez, 26 June 1993, but lost it via decision in Johannesberg, 30 October 1993, to Orzubek Nazarov.

After Pernell Whitaker's vacation of the throne he had occupied so nobly and with such credit, the WBC predictably held its own tournament. Miguel Angel Gonzalez won the claim by ninth-round TKO over Colombia's Wilfrido Rocha, Mexico City, 24 August 1992. The IBF responded with its own plans. Recognized contenders Freddie Pendleton and Tracy Spann met at Reno, Nevada, 29 August 1992, only to butt heads, and cause a cut eye: the match was stopped in the second round and declared a technical draw. The return bout in Atlantic City, 10 January 1993, gave Pendleton his claim via unanimous decision.

Presently (March 1994) Mexico's Miguel A Gonzalez, undefeated in thirty-one fights with twenty-five knockouts, holds the WBC claim. Olzubek Nazarov of Russia, undefeated in eighteen fights with fourteen KOs, holds the WBA claim. America's Fred Pendleton holds the IBF claim with thirty-five wins, (twenty-three by KO), eighteen losses and four draws. Nobody seriously cares who has the WBO 'title'. Wouldn't it be nice if there could be a co-operative elimination tournament to determine the true champion? Of course, that isn't going to happen.

Just supposing this took place, though, one would be inclined to pick Miguel A Gonzalez as being the best of the current crop of lightweights, though one needs to know more about Olzubok Nazarov. Leading contender Rafael Ruelas of America, who has had thirty-nine wins (thirty-one by KO) and only one loss, is also clearly a man to be reckoned with. It is to be hoped that out of all this jumble and mess, a single

champion will emerge with the authority of a Duran, a
Chavez or a Whitaker.

The lightweight division, with such a long and noble
history, deserves better than its current state of undistinguished confusion, although it has survived similar states
before. Unsatisfactory anarchy has never continued long here.
It is only a matter of time before we can once more rejoice in
the triumphs of these great little men as their lightning strikes
to make a far better match than that of two slow, dull and
plodding heavyweights. 'Lightweights, my lightweights,
where have you gone?' Indeed. But they will come again.

NOTE TO CHAPTER SIXTEEN

No boxer has proved an undisputed right to the world
lightweight championship ever since Pernell Whitaker
vacated the throne, in April 1992. Here are the claims:

TRADITIONALIST
    Pernell Whitaker 1990–2 (relinquished title).
    Title Vacant.

WBC

    Pernell Whitaker 1989–92 (relinquished title).
    Miguel Angel Gonzalez 1992–present.

WBA
    Edwin Rosario 1989–90.
    Juan Nazario 1990.
    Pernell Whitaker 1990–2 (relinquished title).
    Joey Gamache 1992.
    Tony Lopez 1992–3.
    Dingaan Thobela 1993.
    Orzubek Nazarov 1993–present.

IBF

    Pernell Whitaker 1989–92 (relinquished title).
    Freddie Pendleton 1993–present.

17

Who Was the Greatest?

The question of who was the greatest, and in what order the men should be placed, perpetually engages the attention of boxing aficionados. It is hard enough to address this question when considering the heavyweights, though at least we do not have the problems here of movement from one weight division to another. Greatest? By what standard? And what are our rules of measurement to be? This author intends to ignore the impact made by boxers outside the ring, no matter what their merits, and to concentrate on sheer boxing ability.

Even this does not simplify the question. Who is to be ranked? Henry Armstrong, for instance, is usually ranked among the top three all-time welterweights, competing with Sugar Ray Robinson and Sugar Ray Leonard. His venture into the lightweight championship consisted of a close decision win and a close decision loss against Lou Ambers. No one doubts that Armstrong was among the greatest of all time

– but where does he rank among the lightweights? Can we rate featherweight Jem Driscoll, who never won the title but who beat top American lightweights? What about Owen Moran, conqueror of Battling Nelson, who beat Ad Wolgast severely, only to be savagely fouled and unfairly halted? Heaven knows how many alphabet titles that man might have won today.

There are three ways of structuring this matter. One is to rank all the men who ever had a claim to be lightweight champion of the world. The second is to rank all the men who boxed at the lightweight limit of 135 pounds. The third is to rank the champions who were primarily lightweights, whatever other adventures they may have had. Let us have a go at all three.

What can we use as our tools of measurement? What constitutes sound and unsound data? For instance, let us take the case of Joe Gans. Nat Fleischer, 'Mr. Boxing', who founded the legendary journal *The Ring* in 1922, saw all the best men for over half a century and declared that the best were Joe Gans, Battling Nelson and Benny Leonard. Obviously one respects his opinion but can we see the evidence for ourselves? To my knowledge, there is no video of Joe Gans boxing. I have seen one of Battling Nelson fighting Owen Moran and this is quite a revelation. It is an absolutely splendid contest, with Moran boxing exquisitely and Nelson soaking up enough punishment to kill an average champion, before Moran finishes the man. One can see both these men doing well in today's ring. Unfortunately, I have never seen a film of Benny Leonard fighting. So how can we make sensible comparisons? Let's refer to a statement made by Muhammad Ali:

Boxing is boxing. Some was good, some wasn't, some today can beat those who fought then, some then could beat those who fight today. They're all gone and there's no way to prove it. It's just hearsay and just hypothetical, and all I say is that all the time they were good. Probably style change a little, more dancing and more rhythm and more speed ... Running is the same, punching the bag is the same, jumping rope's the same, resting, and going to camp, following the dietary laws. Clean living is the same.

Obviously it is very hard to argue with Muhammad Ali who as usual is talking clear common sense here: but it doesn't wholly sort out the matter. For example, anyone who watches the draw between Henry Armstrong and Ceferino Garcia back in the Thirties can't help feeling that the Roberto Duran who decisioned Sugar Ray Leonard could have powdered the pair of them. The Olympic Games have given us scientific measurements of athletic achievement. Every time, records are broken. Men and women can run faster, jump higher, lift heavier weights and perform feats considered impossible a generation ago. Are we seriously expected to believe that the sport of boxing is the sole exception to this rule?

It has been said that the arts of the master craftsmen such as Joe Gans have been lost, but I find this very hard to believe. That Gans was extraordinarily talented is not in dispute. A generation later, world heavyweight champion Gene Tunney was concurring with the general view of calling Gans 'the Old Master'. Nevertheless, his contemporary, Jack Blackburn, was teaching his secrets in the gyms of America during the 1930s to men such as the great Joe Louis. Ray Arcel taught everything he saw from the Thirties through the Eighties. Angelo Dundee learned from all the fighters of the Forties, then trained his men to use new styles. All these lessons passed through the gyms and trainers were sometimes astonished by the innovations of their pupils.

The idea that men were then much tougher does not stand up to close inspection. Battling Nelson, sometimes fighting once a week, was probably tougher than the average pugilist of today, but then he was tougher than the average pugilist of yesteryear. Is it arguable that he was tougher than another child of the slums, Roberto Duran? Mentally, maybe, if we regard the second Leonard–Duran go, but physically? Doubtful. If all athletes nowadays show measurable powers of greater endurance at the Olympic Games than their predecessors, again it is unlikely that boxers are the sole exception. One also wonders if Battling Nelson could lay a glove on Pernell Whitaker.

Attempts have been made to sort out this contentious matter by using a computer. It has been tried with the heavyweight champions and, in realistic terms, it has proved a disastrous failure. A computer depends solely upon those who feed in its programmes. Garbage in means garbage out. A programme fed into a computer is simply an item of personal opinion.

What data, then, can we sensibly use? I can only recommend reason, observation, logic and close study of the words of the boxers themselves, and of the trainers and reporters intimately involved with them.

Obviously the matter is open to debate but I think that the greatest lightweight champion of all time was Roberto Duran. Given what has been said earlier about improved athleticism and the learning of new techniques, I cannot see Joe Gans or Benny Leonard keeping him away. One thinks of Benny Leonard tricking Lew Tendler out of a potential victory by telling him to keep his punches up when Tendler paralysed his legs with a body shot. Lew stopped to argue and lost the fight. Duran would not have stopped to debate the matter. When a battered Leonard dared Ritchie Mitchell to 'come in and mix it', Mitchell, suspecting a trick, stayed away. Duran would have seen a hurt boxer trying it on and would have gone right in to mix it and to finish his stricken foe.

Battling Nelson was notoriously open and easy to hit; and any man hit by Duran went down sooner or later. Nelson could never have tagged the elusive and cunning Duran. Duran v Ike Williams? That would have been quite a fight, as it would have been against Tony Canzoneri, Barney Ross,

Lou Ambers or Henry Armstrong; but I stick to my view that the best men of today have the edge over the best men of yesteryear. Some would of course support the claims of Julio Cesar Chavez. Certainly he is among the all-time greats but one cannot see him doing a Duran and going the fifteen-round distance with Marvelous Marvin Hagler at middleweight championship level. Pernell Whitaker would have had a good chance against Duran but I believe that the latter in his prime would have half-murdered Whitaker's leg speed with his body shots.

Tentatively, therefore, I propose the following lists so as to spark off fruitful debate. For the greatest boxers who have ever held the lightweight championship of the world, fighting at that weight: (1) Roberto Duran (2) Pernell Whitaker (3) Julio Cesar Chavez (4) Henry Armstrong (5) Benny Leonard (6) Joe Gans (7) Ike Williams (8) Carlos Ortiz (9) Barney Ross (10) Tony Canzoneri. My list for every man who has ever fought at the 135 pound limit is the same. On the third, if we remove Armstrong and Ross as natural welterweights and concentrate simply upon the champions who were primarily lightweights, then it reads: (1) Roberto Duran (2) Pernell Whitaker (3) Julio Cesar Chavez (4) Benny Leonard (5) Joe Gans (6) Ike Williams (7) Carlos Ortiz (8) Tony Canzoneri (9) Joe Brown (10) Battling Nelson, although uncrowned contender Owen Moran was visibly better. Nor should we ever forget Lou Ambers and Alexis Arguello.

Obviously lists of this nature will never be sorted out to everyone's satisfaction and it is best simply to enjoy discussing the issue by civilized argument. One matter, though, is beyond dispute. These lightweight kings gave the sporting public greater thrills than all but the best of the heavyweights.

Appendix I

The 'Junior' and 'Super' Lightweight Championships

What exactly are 'junior' and 'super' titles? Once upon a time, there were eight sensible weight divisions, each one with a champion. The man in the street could tell you their names. Now there are sixteen weight divisions and some of them have more than three title claimants. Any sane person could be forgiven for losing count of all the 'champions', but sixty-four would not be too inaccurate an estimate.

A cynic might observe that if a lightweight misses his dinner, he goes down to junior lightweight, but if he has double pie and beans followed by suet pudding and custard, he goes up to super lightweight. The super lightweight/junior welterweight limit is 140 pounds. The lightweight limit is 135 pounds. The junior lightweight/super featherweight limit is 130 pounds. Why did these extra divisions, in which so many of our excellent lightweights have fought with distinction, come into existence?

The answer, of course, is money. People would rather pay to see a title contest than a non-title contest. It also makes for an easier sale of TV rights. Many American television viewers appear to think that the WBC, the WBA, the IBF and even the WBO have the same credibility as the National League and the American League in American sports, but this is hardly the case. The National League and the American Leagues co-operate over the Super-Bowl to find out which is the best team. Unfortunately, this doesn't happen in boxing.

Not all recent weight innovations, however, have been bad. To me, it makes absolute sense to have introduced the cruiserweight division, which the WBA calls 'junior heavyweight'. The light-heavyweight limit was 175 pounds. Most heavyweights these days are over 210 pounds. It is surely right, therefore, to have a 175–190 pound weight division. But were all the other new divisions really necessary?

This matter can be argued, for the precedent of the junior lightweight division goes back to 1921, when big-time interest in the sport was rapidly reviving. Johnny Dundee, known as 'the Scotch wop', won this new championship on a foul in the fifth round against George 'KO' Chaney. After three defences by decision, he dropped the title on points to Jack Bernstein, 1923, but won it back on points seven months later. He also won the world featherweight championship 1923–4. Steve 'Kid' Sullivan decisioned Dundee to take the increasingly valued junior lightweight crown, 1924, but lost it on 1 April 1925 to a man he had previously KO'd, Mike Ballarino. After two defences, Ballarino was hammered to the canvas in the same year by Tod Morgan. Nat Loubet, who was Nat Fleischer's son-in-law and who followed him as editor of *The Ring*, called Morgan 'a phenomenal fighter'.

Certainly, outstanding men have fought at the junior lightweight limit. The division's first champion, Johnny Dundee, for instance, had no less than 322 recorded bouts.

Tod Morgan had a remarkable career that lasted twenty-two years, incorporating no less than 205 recorded professional contests. It is a pity that he never fought for, or had the opportunity to fight for, the world lightweight championship; but he successfully defended his junior lightweight title four times 1925–9. Benny Bass, world featherweight champion 1927–8, wiped him away in two rounds, 1929, but was in turn halted in seven by the legendary Kid Chocolate.

This stylish Cuban was willing to fight anybody, anywhere, anytime. He was sufficiently audacious to challenge the great Tony Canzoneri for both the lightweight and junior welterweight titles, losing a fair but close one over fifteen rounds. He bounced back to win New York Commission recognition as world featherweight champion, 1932, in addition to holding the junior lightweight title 1931–3. As we have seen, syphilis severely affected his fighting abilities; and after two successful defences, he was stopped in the seventh, Philadelphia, 1933, by Frankie Klick. Klick never defended his title, everybody lost interest and it passed away without any regrets.

There was an endeavour to revive this crown, 6 December 1949, when Sandy Saddler decisioned Orlando Zulueta, 'the fighter with knives in his gloves', at Cleveland, Ohio. Saddler, an all-time great and featherweight champion of the world 1948–9 and 1950–7, beat the great Willie Pep three times out of four and knocked out 103 men. He also defended his junior lightweight title against future world lightweight champion Lauro Salas, 1950 (KO–9) and Diego Sosa, 1951 (KO–2), after which he abandoned it.

Eight years passed with no interest in the matter. Then, on 29 July 1959, Harold Gomes of Providence, Rhode Island, decisioned Paul Jorgensen to take the title. A year later, 16 March 1960, he was knocked out by Gabriel 'Flash' Elorde, Manila. Elorde, who had been halted in a world featherweight challenge by Sandy Saddler (TKO–13), repeated his victory over Gomes five months later. Elorde was truly formidable at the 130 pound weight limit. He defended his title nineteen times in the ensuing six years and came a cropper only when he tried to move up to the lightweight championship. In 1964 and 1966, both his challenges were turned back by Carolos Ortiz by first-round TKO on each occasion. Finally, Elorde lost his title in Tokyo, 1967, on points to Yoshiaki Numata.

It is best at this point simply to give the tables and append comments.

THE JUNIOR LIGHTWEIGHT CHAMPIONSHIP OF THE WORLD

Johnny Dundee 1921–3.
Jack Bernstein 1923.
Johnny Dundee 1923–4.
Steve 'Kid' Sullivan 1924–5.
Mike Ballarino 1925.
Tod Morgan 1925–9.
Benny Bass 1929–31.
Kid Chocolate 1931–3.
Frankie Klick 1933 (relinquished title).
Sandy Saddler 1949–51 (relinquished title).
Harold Gomes 1959–60.
Gabriel 'Flash' Elorde 1960–7.
Yoshiaki Numata 1967.
Hiroshi Kobayashi 1967.

The newly formed WBC introduced confusion into this simplicity by stripping Kobayashi of his title for refusing a rematch with Ireneo 'Rene' Barrientos, with whom he had boxed a draw in 1968. The WBA continued to support Kobayashi's claim, which he defended via decisions four times in Tokyo. Venezuela's Alfredo Marcano TKO'd Kobayashi, 29 July 1971, Aomori, Japan, in the tenth. The WBA lineage follows:

Alfredo Marcano 1971–2.
Ben Villaflor 1972–3.
Kuniaki Shibata 1973.
Ben Villaflor 1973–6.

Villaflor of the Philippines won back the title with a sensational 1st round knockout over Shibata and defended it five times, before dropping it via decision to Samuel Serrano of Puerto Rico in San Juan. Serrano was distinguished at this weight, for he defended his claim ten times, lost it to Japan's Yasutsune Uehara (KO–6), won it back via decision and enjoyed three more successful defences before being KO'd in eight rounds by the distinguished Roger Mayweather.

Samuel Serrano 1976–80.
Yasutsune Uehara 1980–1.
Samuel Serrano 1981–3.
Roger Mayweather 1983–4.
Rocky Lockridge 1984–5.
Wilfredo Gomez 1985–6

Gomez is generally recognized as being among the all-time greats. He had defended his WBC junior featherweight title no less than seventeen times 1977–82, every time by KO. This included victories over great bantamweight champions Carlos Zarate and Lupe Pintor. Moving up to challenge for the WBC featherweight championship, he was stopped by the immortal Salvador Sanchez in the eighth (1981), but rebounded to take the WBC title off formidable Juan LaPorte via decision (1984). Azumah Nelson halted his brief reign nine months later by eleventh-round TKO. The Junior Lightweight win over Rocky Lockridge was soon enough followed a year later by a nine-round TKO at the hands of Alfredo Layne.

Alfredo Layne 1986.
Brian Mitchell 1986–91.

Mitchell, of South Africa, enjoyed a distinguished reign. He defended his title thirteen times, with five KOs, one technical decision and two draws. In 1991, the WBA chose to strip him of his crown for the 'offence' of fighting the IBF champion, Tony Lopez in an endeavour to bring some sorely required clarity to the matter. This did not occur, since the result was a draw. Five months later, however, Mitchell decisioned Lopez to take the IBF crown and then retired, March 1992.

Genaro Hernandez 1992–present.

This man's record presently stands at twenty-nine wins (fourteen by KO), no losses and one draw. Let us turn to the WBC lineage:

Ireneo 'Rene' Barrientos 1969–70.
Yoshiaki Numata 1970–1 (WBA JL king 1967).
Ricardo Arrendondo 1971–4.
Kuniaki Shibata 1974–5 (WBA JL king 1973; WBC F king 1970–2).
Alfredo Escalera 1975–8.
Alexis Arguello 1978–80 (relinquished title).

Escalera was a solid title-holder, defending his claim twelve times, six by KO, but he was no match for Arguello, who twice halted him in the thirteenth round and with whose exemplary career we have already dealt.

Rafael 'Bazooka' Limon 1980–1.
Cornelius Boza-Edwards 1981.
Rolando Navarrete 1981–2.
Rafael 'Bazooka' Limon 1982.
Bobby Chacon 1982–3 (WBC F king 1974–5).

All these men were sensational performers who fought each other repeatedly in tremendous ring wars. But on 27 June 1983, the WBC moved in mysterious ways to deprive Chacon of his title. This went to Hector Camacho, whom we have met, when he stopped 'Bazooka' Limon.

Hector Camacho 1983–4 (relinquished title).
Julio Cesar Chavez 1984–7 (relinquished title).
Azumah Nelson 1988–present (WBC F king 1984–8).

Nelson, in common with Camacho and Chavez, is a ring legend. Having defended his WBC featherweight championship seven times, he has gone on to defend the WBC junior lightweight crown eight times. His only losses have been to the great Salvador Sanchez in his first endeavour to capture the featherweight crown; and to the great Pernell Whitaker in a 1990 attempt to take the lightweight throne. Most traditionalists regard him as being the true 130 pound champion.

There is still the IBF to be reckoned with. Here is the lineage:

Hwan-Kil Yuh 1984–5.
Lester Ellis 1985.
Barry Michael 1985–7.
Rocky Lockridge 1987–8 (WBA JL king 1984–5).
Tony Lopez 1988–9.
Juan Molina 1989–90.
Tony Lopez 1990–1.
Brian Mitchell 1991 (WBA JL king 1987–91; relinquished title).
Juan Molina 1992–present.

It would be good for the division in particular and the sport in general if an elimination tournament could be organized between the various champions, but given the fragmented and factional financial interests of the powers that be, this seems unlikely.

The super-lightweight or junior welterweight championship, in which so many lightweight champions have fought with distinction, came into existence under curious circumstances in 1922. Mike Collins, editor of the long defunct magazine *The Boxing Blade*, wanted to promote the fighter he managed, 'Pinkie' Mitchell, who was too heavy for the lightweights and too light for the welterweights. He invited his readers to enter a competition to decide the issue and they voted for Pinkie: surprise, surprise. Pinkie held his crown for four years by the simple expedient of not defending it; but was eventually vanquished by a worthy contender, Mushy Callahan. Callahan lost the title to England's outstanding Jackie 'Kid' Berg in London. Lord Lonsdale arose at ringside to protest that there was no such title: but Berg's whirlwind performances in America, where he defended his claim nine times in fifteen months, gave the matter some credibility. Berg was a superb fighter and it was his misfortune that he never held one of the major championships despite being good enough to win one. Eventually he was stopped by the legendary lightweight champion Tony Canzoneri. The record reads:

Myron 'Pinkie' Mitchell 1922–6.
Mushy Callahan 1926–30.
Jackie 'Kid' Berg 1930–1.
Tony Canzoneri 1931–2.
Johnny Jadick 1932–3.
Battling Shaw 1933.
Tony Canzoneri 1933.
Barney Ross 1933–5 (relinquished title).

The division passed into inactivity until 1946 when Tippy Larkin twice decisioned Willie Joyce; and it was not revived again until Carlos Ortiz KO'd Kenny Lane in 1959. As we have noted, Ortiz did not consider this to be a true championship, though he did defend it successfully twice.

Tippy Larkin 1946.

Carlos Ortiz 1959–60.
Duilio Loi 1960–2.
Eddie Perkins 1962.
Duilio Loi 1962–3 (relinquished title).
Roberto Cruz 1963.
Eddie Perkins 1963–5.
Carlos Hernandez 1965–6.
Sandro Lopopolo 1966–7.
Paul Takeshi Fujii 1967–8.

At this point there was a falling out, as usual, between the WBA and the WBC. The WBC stripped Fujii of his crown by agreeing to fight leading contender Nicolino Loche instead of the lesser known man it advocated, Pedro Adigue. This high-handed action disgusted traditionalists who continued to follow the WBA lineage.

Nicolino Loche 1968–72.
Alfonso 'Peppermint' Frazier 1972.
Antonio Cervantes 1972–6.
Wilredo Benitez 1976 (relinqushed title).
Antonio Cervantes 1976–80.

Cervantes was very fine at this weight, for apart from his decision loss to Benitez, he defended his crown seventeen times, with twelve KOs. It was certainly no disgrace to lose on points to Benitez, who went on to win the WBC welterweight championship and the WBC junior middle-weight title. When Cervantes finally lost, it was to the scintillating Aaron 'The Hawk' Pryor. Pryor stormed through all the contenders, winning all his ten defences, eight by KO, including two brilliant victories, as noted, over superb lightweight champion Alexis Arguello. He retired without ever having been defeated in his ring career. Unfortunately, he snorted most of his ring earnings up his nose and was soon reduced to being a shadow of his former self.

Aaron Pryor 1980–3 (relinquished title).
Johnny Bumphus 1984.
Gene Hatcher 1984–5.
Ubaldo Sacco 1985–6.
Patrizio Oliva 1986–7.
Juan Martin Coggi 1987–90.
Loreto Garza 1990–1.
Edwin Rosario 1991–2 (WBC L king 1983–4; WBA L king 1986–7).
Akinobu Hiranaka 1992.
Morris East 1992–3.
Juan Martin Coggi 1993–present (WBA JW king 1987–90).

Here follows the WBC lineage:

Pedro Adigue 1968–70.
Bruno Arcari 1970–4 (relinquished title).
Perico Fernandez 1974–5.
Saesek Muangsurin 1975–6.
Miquel Velasquez 1976.
Saesek Muangsurin 1976–8.
Sang Hyun Kim 1978–1980.
Saoul Mamby 1980–2.
Leroy Haley 1982–3.
Bruce Curry 1983–4.
Bill Costello 1984–5.
Lonnie Smith 1985–6.
Rene Arrendondo 1986.
Tsuyoshi Hamada 1986–7.
Rene Arrendondo 1987.
Roger Mayweather 1987–9 (WBA JL king 1983–4).

Bruno Arcari was probably the most distinguished claimant, since he defended his title nine times, five by KO, and retired undefeated. Saesek Muangsurin was possibly the least distinguished, for this former kick-boxer won the title in only his third fight. Saoul Mamby was a good boxer and a widely respected veteran. The same can be said for Roger Mayweather, who was nevertheless destroyed in ten rounds by the then invincible Julio Cesar Chavez. There must be also an honourable mention for 'Lightning' Lonnie Smith whose eighth-round stoppage of tough Billy Costello has been called one of the most beautiful exhibitions of sheer boxing skill ever witnessed at New York's hallowed Madison Square Garden: unfortunately, Smith grew great for only one night.

Chavez defeated Meldrick Taylor to take the IBF crown too and was recognized by traditionalists as the true champion since Aaron Pryor had given up his WBA/traditionalist throne. No one really knows why the IBF withdrew recognition from Chavez but the reasons, if any, are not to its credit. Chavez still kept the WBC belt and defeated both Lonnie Smith and Hector Camacho before his encounter at a higher weight with Pernell Whitaker, as described, and his loss to Frankie Randall.

Julio Cesar Chavez 1989–94.
Frankie Randall 1994.
Julio Cesar Chavez 1994–present.

Randall has presently forty-eight wins, thirty-six by KO, with two losses and one draw.

The IBF, formed 1983–4, of course went its own way, greatly disappointing those who had originally hailed its arrival with high hopes. It recognized Aaron Pryor's return to the ring when he decisioned Nicky Furlano, 22 June 1984, and handed him the belt. Pryor then outpointed Gary Hinton but slid back into wasting himself, declining to defend his claim. The lineage is as follows:

Aaron Pryor 1984–6.
Gary Hinton 1986.
Joe Manley 1986–7.

Terry Marsh 1987–8 (relinquished title).
James 'Buddy' McGirt 1988.
Meldrick Taylor 1988–90.

Owing possibly to the controversial circumstances in which
Taylor lost his title to Chavez, the IBF continued to recognize
Taylor as its champion. After defending it against Primo Ramos
by decision, he vacated this particular throne, won the WBA
welterweight championship against Aaron Davin in 1991 and
lost it in 1992 to Cristo Espana.

Julio Cesar Chavez 1990.
Meldrick Taylor 1990–1 (relinquished title).
Rafael Pineda 1991–2.
Pernell Whitaker 1992–3 (relinquished title).
Charles Murray 1993–present.

Pernell Whitaker proceeded to win WBC and the traditionalist recognition as welterweight champion of the world. With a
record of thirty-four wins, fifteen by KO, one decision loss and
one draw, he is presently regarded as the greatest pound-for-
pound boxer of our time.

Charles Murray has thirty-one wins, nineteen by KO, and
one loss. One would like to see him fight WBA claimant Juan
Martin Coggi, or better still, Frankie Randall, the WBC champion who beat Julio Cesar Chavez and who is therefore recognized by traditionalists. It is a safe bet, though, that common
sense will not prevail.

To conclude, therefore, by answering the questions with
which we started: the junior lightweight/super featherweight
title is for men boxing at 130 pounds. The super lightweight/
junior welterweight/light welterweight title is for men boxing at
140 pounds. The lightweight championship is of course for men
boxing at 135 pounds.

The WBA, WBC and IBF are self-appointed boxing 'authorities' which purport to regulate the sport and which are not

responsible to any national government or international organization such as the United Nations. They do whatever they like, as does the WBO, charge huge 'sanctioning fees' for any contests involving their 'titles', pick the judges and the referee, and regularly strip their champions of their crowns for reasons that have nothing whatsoever to do with anything that has taken place in the ring. No boxer, however good, can hope to make any sort of decent living or secure prominence unless he has a manager or promoter connected to these bodies. Some managers and promoters are so wealthy and influential, having also vital connections with TV networks, that they can dictate their own terms to these alphabet boys. Unfortunately, and in too many cases, the champions are not stripped of their titles but of their money. Money and influence governs the prize-ring; a cynic might say that this has always been the case. Most fighters are honest but most manipulators are not, though there have been and are wonderful exceptions. Meanwhile a gullible public is being sold one lousy swindle after another. Boxing won't die: but its controllers could well poison it through flagrant dishonesty, unfair decisions and sheer crookery. This could lead either to a general call for such a scandal to be banned – which will, as always, merely drive it underground into further sewers of depravity – or else bring about a financial decline, faced with an apathetic public that no longer wishes to be suckered into paying good money for old rope.

For traditionalists, the world lightweight championship is presently vacant; the world junior lightweight championshp is presently held by Azumah Nelson and the world junior welterweight championship is in the hands of Julio Cesar Chavez.

This raises a vital question which may yet save the endangered Noble Art: what exactly is boxing traditionalism?

Appendix II

What is Boxing Traditionalism?

Traditionalism in boxing is:

1 – Having a genuine love of the Noble Art.

2 – Declaring before any contest, no matter what one's personal preferences or bets may be: 'May the best man win.'

3 – Appreciating both the wondrous skills of the intelligent boxer and the magnificent toughness of the rugged fighter.

4 – A determination to keep records that are truthful and exact.

5 – An unwillingness, in commentating to the public, to say any better than one has seen.

6 – The conviction that championships or title claims can only be won or lost in the ring.

7 – The conviction that a man can only lose his championship

or claim to it if he voluntarily relinquishes it, refuses to defend it or is rendered incapable of so doing outside the ring.

8 – The belief that if a championship or title claim becomes vacant, the issue is to be decided by a contest between internationally recognized leading contenders. If there are a number and three or more 'world authorities' hold their own tournaments, then the title should be considered vacant until one recognized claimant clearly beats another.

9 – That the sport should be kept clean and fair, with every possible safety provision for the boxers; including the vital matter that if one boxer is clearly overwhelming the other, the fight should be stopped in favour of the winner.

10 – That all ringside officials such as the referee, judges and timekeeper should be competent and experienced and (preferably) licensed by a legal authority. A medical doctor should always be present.

Adherence to these basic principles was pioneered by Nat Fleischer in 1922 when he founded *The Ring*. Unfortunately, *The Ring* has had some ups and downs since his death, especially on its ratings during the mid-1970s when it was accused of collaboration with promoter Don King. Fortunately, these values can still be found in two magazines today: Bert Sugar's *Boxing Illustrated* (USA) and *Boxing News* (UK).

Appendix III

Record of the World Lightweight Championship 1896–1994

NOTE: This Table of Champions lists in order the winner, the result, loser, the date and the place with the occasional explanatory note.

George 'Kid' Lavigne KO–17 Dick Burge 1.6.1896, London.
Frank Erne W–20 George 'Kid' Lavigne 3.7.1899, Buffalo, NY.
Joe Gans KO–12 Frank Erne 23.3.1900, New York.
Battling Nelson KO–17 Joe Gans 1.7.08, San Francisco.
Ad Wolgast KO–40 Battling Nelson, 22.2.10, Port Richmond, Ca.
Willie Ritchie W–Disq–16 Ad Wolgast, 28.11.12, Daly City, Ca.

Freddie Welsh W–20 Willie Ritchie 7.7.14, London.
Benny Leonard KO–9 Freddie Welsh 28.5.17, New York.
   Leonard relinquished the championship 1925.
Jimmy Goodrich KO–2 Stanislaus Loayza 13.7.25, Long Island, NY.
Rocky Kansas W–15 Jimmy Goodrich 7.12.25, Buffalo, NY.
Sammy Mandell W–10 Rocky Kansas 3.7.26, Chicago.
Al Singer KO–1 Sammy Mandell 17.7.30, New York.
Tony Canzoneri KO–1 Al Singer 17.3.30, New York.
Barney Ross W–15 Tony Canzoneri 26.3.33, Chicago.
   Ross relinquished the championship 1934.
Tony Canzoneri W–15 Lou Ambers 10.5.35, New York.
Lou Ambers W–15 Tony Canzoneri 3.9.36, New York.
Henry Armstrong W–15 Lou Ambers 17.8.38, New York.
Lou Ambers W–15 Henry Armstrong 22.8.39, New York.
Lew Jenkins TKO–3 Lou Ambers 10.5.40, New York.

   There followed different lineages from the New York Commission (NYC) and the National Boxing Association (NBA).

NYC lineage:

Sammy Angott W–15 Lew Jenkins 19.12.41, New York.
   Relinquished the championship 1942.
Beau Jack KO–3 Tippy Larkin 18.12.42, New York.
Bob Montgomery W–15 Beau Jack 21.5.43, New York.
Beau Jack W–15 Bob Montgomery 19.11.43, New York.
Bob Montgomery W–15 Beau Jack 3.3.44, New York.
Ike Williams KO–6 Bob Montgomery 4.8.47, Philadelphia.

NBA lineage:

Sammy Angott W–15 Slugger White 27.10.43, Hollywood.
Juan Zuarita W–15 Sammy Angott 8.3.44, Hollywood.
Ike Williams KO–2 Juan Zuarita 18.4.45, Mexico City.

NYC/NBA/traditionalists:

Jimmy Carter TKO–14 Ike Williams 25.5.51, New York.
Lauro Salas, W–15 Jimmy Carter 14.5.52, Los Angeles.
Jimmy Carter W–15 Lauro Salas, 15.10.52, Chicago.
Paddy De Marco W–15 Jimmy Carter 5.3.54, New York.
Jimmy Carter TKO–15 Paddy DeMarco, 17.11.54, San Francisco.
Wallace 'Bud' Smith W–15 Jimmy Carter 29.6.55, Boston.
Joe Brown W–15 Wallace 'Bud' Smith 24.8.56, New Orleans.
Carlos Ortiz W–15 Joe Brown 21.4.62, Las Vegas.
Ismael Laguna W–15 Carlos Ortiz 10.4.65, Panama City.
Carlos Ortiz W–15 Ismael Laguna 13.11.65, San Juan, Puerto Rico.
Carlos 'Teo' Cruz W–15 Carlos Ortiz 29.6.68, Santo Domingo.
Mando Ramos TKO–11 Carlos 'Teo' Cruz 18.2.69, Los Angeles.
Ismael Laguna TKO–9 Mando Ramos 3.3.70, Los Angeles.

At this juncture, the title was split again. This occurred after Ken Buchanan won a split decision off Laguna, or it could have happened before, depending on which WBC ruling edict one accepts.

WBA/traditionalist recognition:

Ken Buchanan W–15 Ismael Laguna 13.9.71, San Juan.
Roberto Duran TKO–13 Ken Buchanan 26.6.72, New York.

WBC recognition:

Eduardo 'Pedro' Carrasco W–Disq 11 Mando Ramos, 5.11.71, Madrid.
Mando Ramos W–15 Eduardo 'Pedro' Carrasco 18.2.72, Los Angeles.
Erubey 'Chango' Carmona TKO–8 Mando Ramos 15.9.72, Los Angeles.

Rodolfo Gonzalez TKO–12 Chango Carmona 10.11.72, Los Angeles.
Ishimatsu 'Guts' Suzuki KO–9 Rodolfo Gonzalez, 11.4.74, Tokyo.
Esteban DeJesus W–15 Guts Suzuki, 8.5.76, Bayamon, Puerto Rico.
Roberto Duran KO–12 Esteban DeJesus 21.1.78, Las Vegas.

Duran unified the title but needless to say, when he relinquished it on 2.2.79, it once more became fragmented.

WBC recognition:

Jim Watt TKO–12 Alfredo Pitalua, 17.4.79, Glasgow (1981 traditionalist).
Alexis Arguello W–15 Jim Watt 20.6.81, London.

WBA recognition:

Ernesto Espana TKO–13 Claude Noel 16.6.79, Halo Rey, Puerto Rico.
Hilmer Kenty TKO–9 Ernesto Espana, 2.3.80, Detroit.
Sean O'Grady W–15 Hilmer Kenty, 12.4.81, Atlantic City.

Since Jim Watt had previously beaten Sean O'Grady in Glasgow, 1.11.80 via TKO–12, Watt was obviously now the true world lightweight champion in the eyes of traditionalists. It is a matter of common sense. If you lose to the WBC world champion but then beat the WBA world champion, it is obvious who the real champion is.

The O'Grady management then embarked upon a quarrel with the WBA, which resulted in O'Grady giving up his WBA claim and embarking on the short-lived folly of the WAA. We return to the WBA lineage:

Claude Noel W–15 Rodolfo Gonzalez 12.9.81, Atlantic City.
Arturo Frias KO–8 Claude Noel 5.12.81, Las Vegas.
Ray Mancini KO–1 Arturo Frias, 8.5.82, Las Vegas.

Livingstone Bramble TKO–14 Ray Mancini 1.6.84, Buffalo, NY.
Edwin Rosario KO–2 Livingstone Bramble 26.9.86, Miami.
Julio Cesar Chavez TKO–11 Edwin Rosario 21.11.87, Las Vegas.

When former WBA Champion Sean O'Grady lost his spurious 'WAA title' to Andy Ganigan (KO–2, 31.10.81, Little Rock, Arkansas) and Ganigan lost this to traditionalist/WBC champion Alexis Arguello (KO–5, 22.5.82, Las Vegas), it was obvious that Arguello was the true lightweight champion but he relinquished his crown in February 1983. Further WBC recognition follows:

Edwin Rosario W–12 Jose Luis Ramirez 1.5.83, Hato Rey, Puerto Rico.
Jose Luis Ramirez TKO–4 Edwin Rosario 3.11.84, San Juan, Puerto Rico.
Hector Camacho W–12 Jose Luis Ramirez 10.8.85, Las Vegas.

Perhaps one day we shall find out the truth behind the otherwise incomprehensible fact that in April 1987, the WBC withdrew titular recognition from Camacho.

Jose Luis Ramirez W–12 Terrence Alli, 19.7.87, St Tropez, France.
Julio Cesar Chavez TD–11 Jose Luis Ramirez 29.10.88, Las Vegas.

This win, by the WBA champion over the WBC claimant was via TD, 'Technical Decision', a new rule introduced by the WBC, which had also reduced championship bouts from fifteen to twelve rounds. Under this rule, if there is an accident which renders one of the fighters unable to continue, the victory is awarded to whichever fighter is ahead on points at the time.

In this instance, it was ruled that the head-butt which had rendered Jose Luis Ramirez unable to fight on was unintentional and accidental. I have not been able to procure the video of this fight so as to study the matter but all the judges were unanimous in having Chavez ahead at the time, and the boxing press concurred. Chavez was then recognized as undisputed lightweight champion, until he relinquished it in May 1989, by the WBA, the WBC and all traditionalists: but not by the IBF. Its lineage must be recorded:

Charley 'Choo Choo' Brown W–15 Melvin Paul 30.1.84, Atlantic City.
Harry Arroyo TKO–14 Charley 'Choo Choo' Brown 15.4.84, Atlantic City.
Jimmy Paul W–15 Harry Arroyo 6.4.85, Atlantic City.
Greg Haugen W–15 Jimmy Paul 5.12.86, Las Vegas.
Vinny Pazienza W–15 Greg Haugen 7.6.87, Providence, Rhode Island.
Greg Haugen W–15 Vinny Pazienza 6.2.88, Atlantic City.
Pernell Whitaker W–12 Greg Haugen 18.2.89, Hampton, Virginia.

WBC recognition:

Pernell Whitaker W–12 Jose Luis Ramirez 20.8.89, Norfolk, Virginia.

WBA recognition:

Edwin Rosario TKO–6 Anthony Jones 9.7.89, Atlantic City.
Juan Nazario TKO–8 Edwin Rosario 4.4.90, New York.
Pernell Whitaker KO–1 Juan Nazario 11.8.90, Stateline, Nevada.

Obviously Whitaker had unified the world lightweight championship once again: although the WBO begged to differ and this matter is not worthy of serious attention. One should simply note that its fatuous claim passed from Mauricio Acevez (W–12 Amancio Castro 6.5.89, Santa Ana, California): then to Dingaan Thobela (W–12 Mauricio Acevez, Brownsville, Texas 22.9.90) who relinquished this pitiful bauble in June 1992.

Unfortunately, the great Pernell Whitaker chose to vacate the throne he had taken and occupied with such remarkable distinction in pursuit of other crowns, which, as we have seen he won; but it threw the division into renewed confusion that has not yet been resolved.

Nobody other than some miserably ignorant or cynical TV executive gives a damn about who holds the WBO 'claim'. It is merely a device to make money out of the gullible punter. For the record, however, it has to be stated that Giovanni Parisi won this TKO–10 Javier Altamirano (25.9.92, Voghera, Italy). For the record, too, here are the various slices of pie since the departure of Whitaker.

WBC recognition:

Miguel Angel Gonzalez TKO–9, 24.4.92, Mexico City.

WBA recognition:

Tony Lopez TKO–11 Joey Gamache 24.10.92, Portland, Maine.
Dingaan Thobela W–12 Tony Lopez 26.6.93. Sun City, Boph., South Africa.
Orzubek Nazarov W–12 Dingaam Thobela, 30.10.93, Johannesburg.

IBF recognition:

Freddie Pendleton W–12 Tracy Spann 10.1.93, Atlantic City.

We cannot hope for sanity among the 'governing bodies'. But sanity might once more be restored by an excellent boxer.

Traditionalist recognition:

Title vacant.

Bibliographical Note

Readers who wish to pursue further studies in this fascinating matter can be recommended to turn their attention to quite a number of works which have given me so much joy.

For general history, it is hard to beat *A Pictorial History of Boxing* by Sam Andre and Nat Fleischer, updated to 1988 by Andre and Nat Loubet. All of Fleischer's books can be recommended provided that caution is observed. The man who made himself 'Mr Boxing' was a fine ring statistician but those who look for graceful prose will probably be disappointed. Fleischer wrote in the blood 'n'guts sports journalist style of his time. Moreover, he had a marked preference for the fighters of his youth, and although he saw every heavyweight champion from Jeffries to Ali and all the ones in the lower divisions, it is obvious that he feels that the lightweights went downhill after the reign of Benny Leonard. He damns Ike Williams with faint praise and does not appreciate sufficiently either Joe Brown or Carlos Ortiz: though one suspects that he would have loved Roberto Duran and Julio Cesar Chavez.

100 Years of Boxing by Bert R Sugar is another fine, general work on the matter. Sugar has always stood for integrity in the sport, even when it has led to threats and even actions of violence, which he openly treats with contempt. One suspects that this extraordinary man would rather die than surrender any rights as a principal guardian of such integrity as remains to the sport. This guardianship is upheld every month in his *Boxing Illustrated*. Unlike Fleischer, Sugar salts and peppers his writing with acid wit and bitter humour, though he sometimes just chooses to joke.

The Pictorial History of Boxing by Peter Arnold is a valuable addition to the shelves of any aficionado. The text is sound throughout: the choice of pictures is absolutely stunning.

Fleischer and Sugar are outstanding for statistics, though presently the world's greatest has to be Herbert G Goldman, who fortunately gives us his expertise in Bert Sugar's *Boxing Illustrated*. Great Britain's *Boxing News* is also minutely accurate on the matter and always worth reading. This is a publication which has retained its flinty integrity from years dating beyond the First World War. The Guinness *Boxing Who's Who*, compiled by Ian Morrison, can also be warmly recommended.

For the psychology of the boxers, it is impossible to do better than turn to *In This Corner: Forty World Champions Tell Their Stories*, compiled and edited expertly by Peter Heller of New York. As I stated in my *Champions of the Ring: The Lives and Times of Boxing's Heavyweight Heroes*: 'Mr Heller simply lets the boxers speak for themselves – with most illuminating consequences.' Everyone who loves boxing or who enquires into its nature simply has to read this excellent work. It is unique in its excellence.

Autobiographies by the lightweight champions are few and far between and most of them are worthless, since they have been the victim of bad ghosting. However, two Scottish lightweight champions managed to let their voices come through: Ken Buchanan and Jim Watt. In both works one receives an authentic flavour of the ring.

The works of British commentators Harry Carpenter and

Reg Gutteridge are also worth reading, especially on chapters wherein one discerns a genuine and impassioned enthusiasm: at worst, one has wry, dry and appropriate wit. The same is true of O F Snelling's *A Bed-time Book of Boxing*. The sport brings the best out of good writers. Nor should it be forgotten that one of the best works ever to probe its essential nature was *On Boxing* by the celebrated writer of haunting, acutely sensitive novels – Joyce Carol Oates, a woman.